English ❦ Heritage

CONTENTS

ABOUT THIS BOOK 3

WHY USE OBJECTS?
Learning about the present 4
Learning about other times and
other cultures 4
Motivation 4
Developing skills 5
Extending knowledge 5
Developing concepts 5
Will pictures do? 6

LEARNING FROM OBJECTS
Investigating an object 7
Physical features 7
Construction 7
Function 9
Design 9
Value 10

USING OBJECTS ACROSS THE CURRICULUM 14

DEVELOPING SKILLS FOR WORKING WITH OBJECTS
Learning to look 18
Learning to describe 20
Learning to record 20
Learning to ask questions 23
Learning to classify 24
Learning to relate structure
to function 25
Learning to formulate and
test hypotheses 26
Learning to use fragments 26

THINKING ABOUT THINGS
Choosing objects 28
Using replicas and originals 28
Conservation 29
Viewpoint 29
Worth/Value 30
Bias 30
Chronology 31
Continuity, change and progress 31

RESOURCES AND BIBLIOGRAPHY 32

Acknowledgements 36

Boneshaker bicycle, 1869.

ABOUT THIS BOOK

A table is being laid for the evening meal. Its leaves are extended. A white damask cloth is unfolded and laid. Next come the centre-pieces of flowers and candles, and the place settings: crystal glasses, finger-bowls, linen napkins, porcelain dishes, plastic knives and forks.

Plastic knives and forks? This does not fit the image so far. They have the wrong connotations; they are cheap and flimsy and inappropriate for the occasion suggested by the other preparations.

This thought process shows how we assess objects all the time. The description mentions no people, no historical period, no site, only some objects but from it a fairly complex view of a particular occasion and the objects appropriate to it can be built up. All sorts of things may be assumed; some very obvious (such as the social class implied), some more subtle (such as that the occasion seems to be a formal one).

We all use objects as a way of understanding our world. A rucksack, a bowler hat, even a plastic rain-hat, all conjure up images of individual people and their lives.

This book aims to:

■ show how the ability to interpret objects aids our understanding of the world

■ show that specialist knowledge is not essential to learn from objects

■ help teachers to make use of objects in the classroom and at sites

■ make objects central to the curriculum not simply classroom decorations

■ show cross-curricular applications and teaching techniques

Groups studying art, religious education, history, geography, technology, maths, sciences and English can all profit: learning from objects need not necessarily be a history-based activity. A new object could be used for a historical end, or a historical object for a contemporary one. For instance, take any leather shoe. It can become the starting-point in a study of the leather industry, shoemaking techniques, travel, trade, health, costs and values, the nature of historical survival, the effects of wear and ageing; it can generate a detective story identifying the owner of the shoe, a discussion on geographical differences in clothing requirements, differences between male and female shoes, adult and children's shoes or formal, work, leisure and sport shoes, a comparison of human with animal or bird feet, and so on.

Objects cross curricular boundaries: when looking at a sewing-machine, for example, an engineer sees a marriage of design and function, an artist sees a pattern of forms and colours, one historian sees a stage in the changing economic status of women, another the introduction of a machine to produce what was formerly handmade, a needleworker sees a tool and a salesman sees a marketing context.

This book is as much about classroom-based learning as it is about visits to sites, museums and galleries, which is where people tend to think of studying objects. Objects for educational use need not be rare and often the greatest benefits come from using things commonly found in the classroom or home. The book offers a method of analysing objects that, once understood, can be applied at any site or museum. Teachers can make the visit support more than one subject area, which may help timetabling and finances.

In the book we concentrate on artefacts rather than natural objects: artefacts are objects made by people. They are all around us. They can be as small as a pin or as large as a building.

A child's leather boot of about 1900.

WHY USE OBJECTS?

There are things which you can gain only from a study of objects, and things which are much better studied through objects than in any other way.

LEARNING ABOUT THE PRESENT

A major benefit of object-based rather than word-based learning is a greater appreciation of the role of 'things' themselves in our own lives. Things form our world and are as significant to us as language for comprehending it; they aid us in obtaining food, water, warmth and shelter and they figure prominently in everyday activities such as communication, family life, religion, work, art and entertainment. Teaching methods traditionally have concentrated on book- and word-based exercises which ask children to read or write in response. They do not often seem to require children to learn from 'things'.

LEARNING ABOUT OTHER TIMES AND OTHER CULTURES

A further benefit is that an understanding of how to interpret objects creates positive links between today's pupils and other societies throughout the world past or present. They will be able to see problems similar to our own, such as preparation of food or means of locking things away, tackled and solved with ingenuity, elegance and differing degrees of success.

If you can understand objects you can also explore the lives of people who provide no permanent written information about themselves (the urban poor, babies, prehistoric people, rural nomads) and of people whose language you do not read or speak.

MOTIVATION

Objects have a remarkable capacity to motivate. They develop the 'need to know' which will first spark children's interest, then their curiosity or creativity, and then stimulate their research. Handling objects is a form of active learning that engages children in a way that other methods often fail to do. Objects provide a concrete experience that aids or illuminates abstract thought. Interest in them, and their power to motivate, is cumulative so that as pupils learn they put themselves in a position of wanting to learn more.

Objects also provide creative and emotional stimulus. They provide material for art, imaginative writing and drama. They provide examples of how ideas and feelings can be expressed in ways other than through words. Objects are real rather than abstract, and thus they aid the

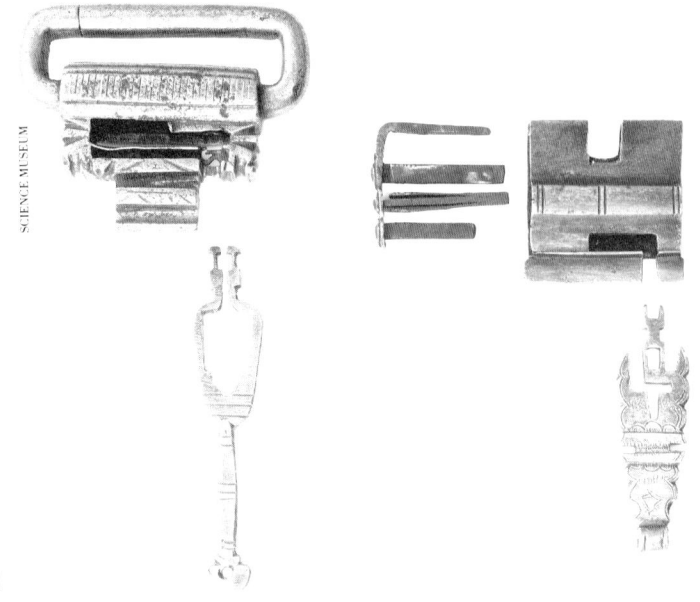

Persian padlocks from the seventeenth or eighteenth century.

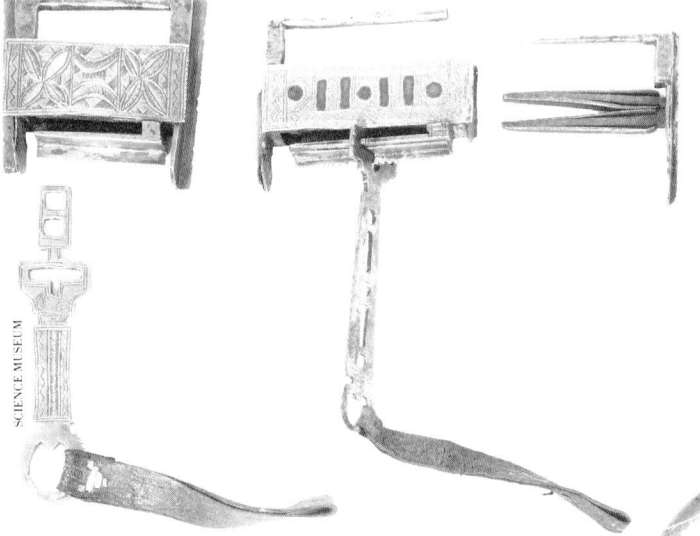

North African padlocks.

Twentieth-century British padlock.

memory: physical sensations, experiences and emotions may remain much longer in the mind than word-gained facts or ideas.

Objects are attention grabbing. Here a class from Edenham High School, Croydon, embarks on a musical instrument study session.

Everyone can use objects. Children who for whatever reason do not read, write or speak English easily, or those with learning difficulties, will often relate well to objects. Whereas the range of reading and writing ability within a class can divide it across a very wide spectrum, the range of ability in dealing with objects will divide them much less. Teachers will be able to set activities at which most children will succeed and remove a barrier to learning.

DEVELOPING SKILLS

The skills which can be developed by using objects include:

■ locating, recognising, identifying, planning

■ handling, preserving, storing

■ observing and examining

■ discussing, suggesting, estimating, hypothesising, synthesising, predicting, generalising, assessing influence

■ experimenting, deducing, comparing, concluding, evaluating

■ relating structure to function, classifying, cataloguing

■ recording through writing, drawing, labelling, photographing, taping, filming, computing

■ responding, reporting, explaining, displaying, presenting, summarising, criticising

EXTENDING KNOWLEDGE

The fields of knowledge specifically developed by using objects include:

■ different materials and what they were used for

■ techniques and vocabulary of construction and decoration

■ the social, historic and economic context within which items featured

■ the physical effects of time

■ the meaning of symbolic forms

■ the way people viewed their world

■ the existence and nature of particular museums, sites, galleries and collections

■ symbol, pattern, colour

■ 'appropriateness', for example the use of rucksacks compared to handbags

■ appreciation of cultural values

There are differences between the sorts of knowledge to be gained from written sources and from objects. In objects we encounter ideas and information which either are not or cannot be expressed effectively in writing or speech – not only the forms, colours and effects of visual arts, but also personal fantasies, idioms of taste, unspoken significances, customs or even prejudices. Medieval travellers describing unusual animals to those who had not seen them found the task daunting, as shown by the attempts of illustrators to convey the animal. Medieval churches and cathedrals, with their vast spaces and spires towering above ordinary dwellings, were physical symbols representing religious awe and religious devotion in ways that could not easily be expressed in words. Queen Victoria would never have announced on an everyday basis her view of herself and Albert as Anglo-Saxons, yet this is how she chose to have them both portrayed on Albert's mausoleum, as a romantic expression of their union – she was the Angle, he the Saxon.

DEVELOPING CONCEPTS

Concepts developed from the study of objects include:

■ chronology, change, continuity and progress

■ design as a function of use, availability of materials and appearance

- aesthetic quality
- typicality, bias, survival
- fashion, style and taste
- original, fake, copy
- heritage, collection, preservation, conservation

WILL PICTURES DO?

In almost every case it is possible to learn something from pictures or descriptions of objects. However, the following aspects will always be lost:

- detail
- exact colouring
- sensations of smell, awe, location, etc. associated with the object
- size, scale, weight, mass
- tactile evidence of textures, temperatures, shape, manufacture
- the three-dimensional design of an object
- 'feeling of age' compared to the newness of a reproduction; the concept of an original

There are some problems in using objects. Sometimes pupils are disappointed if they do not immediately find out what the object is called and/or what it does. Conversely, once children know the name of an object, they are often tempted to dismiss it and overlook the information and ideas which it contains. Familiar objects, too, can be dismissed as having nothing to offer. The questions 'What is this?' and 'How old is it?' are likely to close down the discussion. This book suggests methods of dealing with these problems.

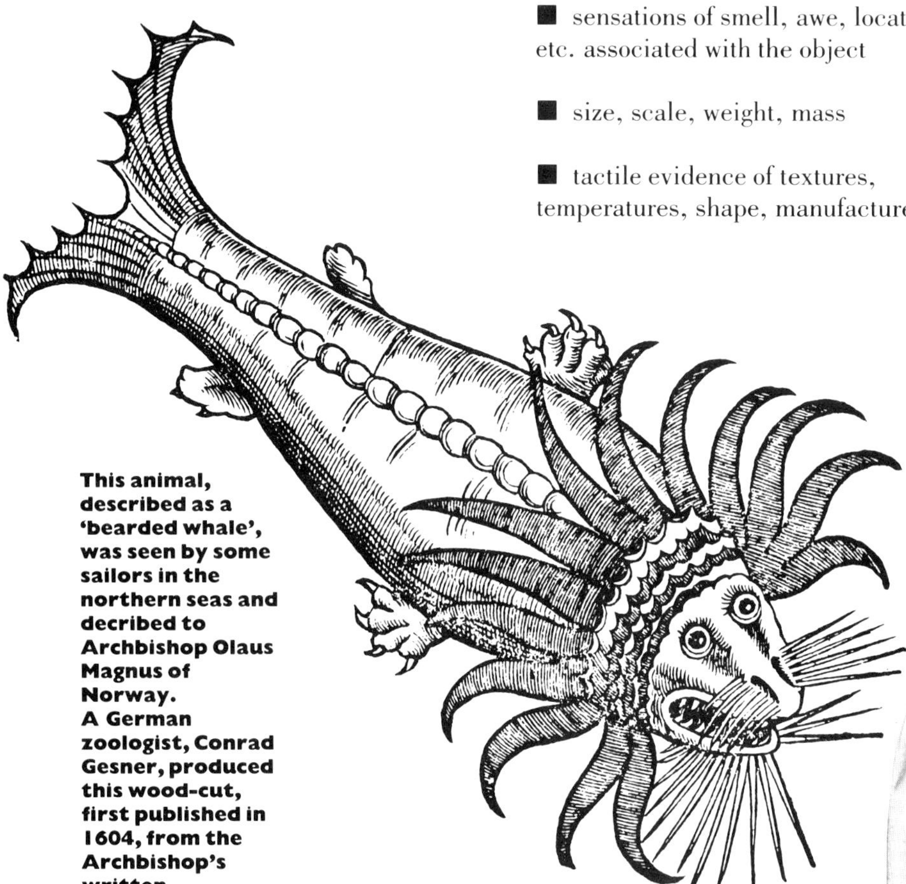

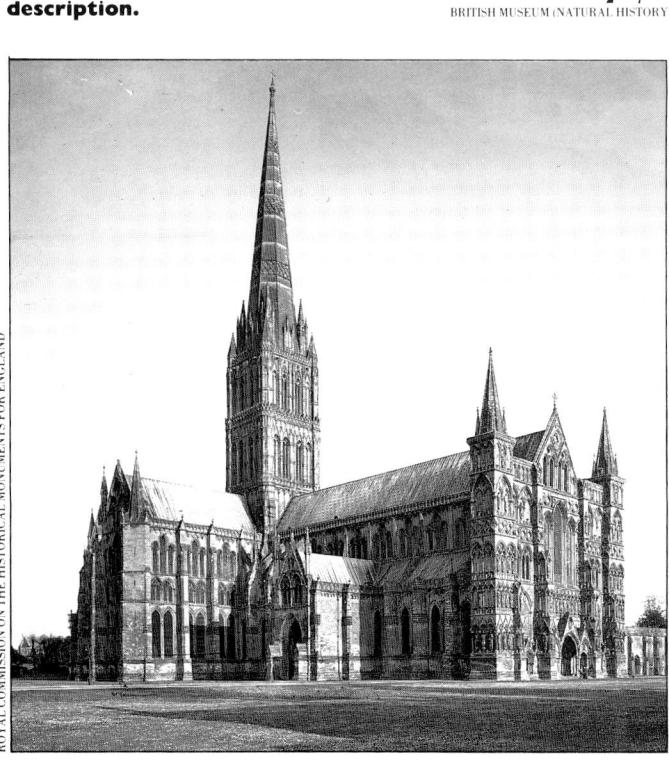

This animal, described as a 'bearded whale', was seen by some sailors in the northern seas and decribed to Archbishop Olaus Magnus of Norway. A German zoologist, Conrad Gesner, produced this wood-cut, first published in 1604, from the Archbishop's written description.

BRITISH MUSEUM (NATURAL HISTORY)

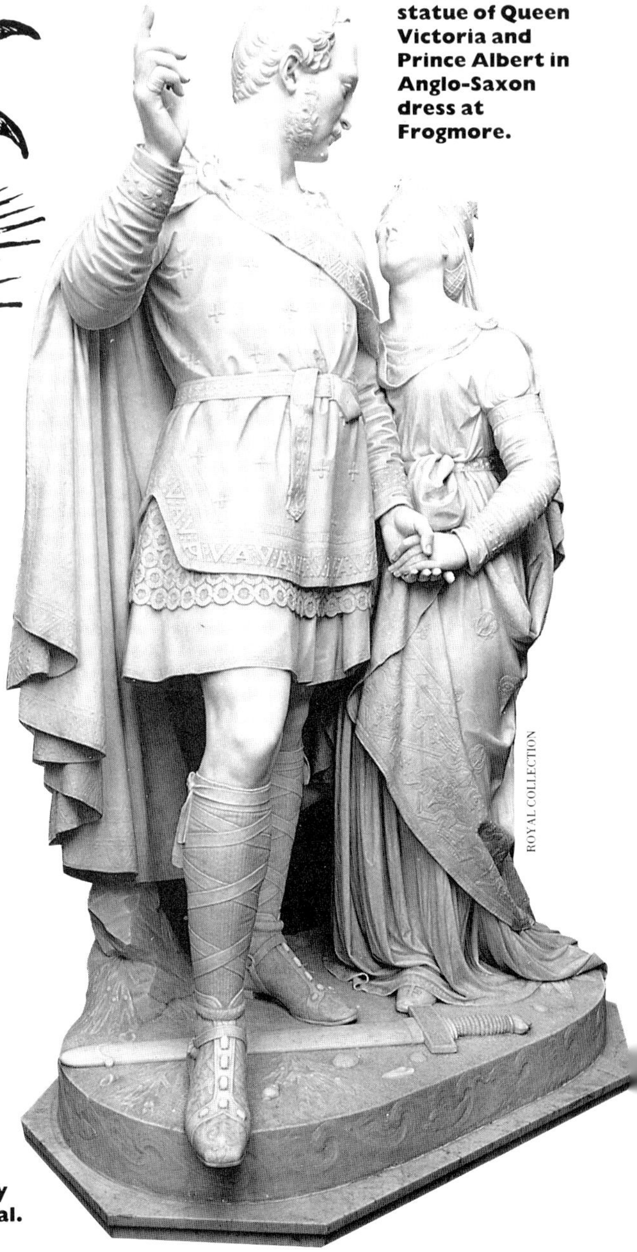

William Theed's statue of Queen Victoria and Prince Albert in Anglo-Saxon dress at Frogmore.

ROYAL COLLECTION

Salisbury Cathedral.

ROYAL COMMISSION ON THE HISTORICAL MONUMENTS FOR ENGLAND

LEARNING FROM OBJECTS

The most mundane object can be made to reveal a range of information if we ask the right questions of it. Take the chair you are sitting on. Is it comfortable? Why? (Or alternatively, why not?) What is it made of? How do you know? Why do you think those particular materials were chosen? What does the chair smell of? What do these smells tell you about it? Has it ever been repaired? How? Why? Is it clean? Who cleans it, and what do they use? Is it decorated in any way? Does it match anything else in the room? Why are you sitting on this particular chair? Was it the only one available or did you choose to sit on it? Why? Who bought the chair? Where did it come from? Why did they choose this particular one? Is it the same as or different from the other chairs in the room? Are the other chairs being used for other purposes? Have you looked underneath the chair yet, or run your fingers down the side of it? Does this alter any of your answers?

Now try adding another ten questions of your own. Don't worry about the order or value of your questions at this stage; the point is to realise how diverse a range of questions a fairly ordinary household object can raise and how much the answers can tell you about your own society, its tastes, preferences, aesthetics, design sense, level of craftsmanship, standard of living, or technological level.

Looking, handling and exploring is the first stage in analysing any artefact. From this will spring a whole host of questions and these questions will fall into different groups according to which aspect of the artefact they are concerned with. Some of the questions about the chair dealt with sensory response to the object, some focused on its physical character, others on its design and decoration, and others on the people who used it or how it was made.

This diagram suggests a method of investigating an object. It identifies the key areas to consider when examining objects and the types of questions to ask. In using a scheme like this in the classroom you should aim to bring children to a position where they can use this method independently and without prompting. This will take time; children will need to be introduced to the process gradually. The sections that follow examine the key areas in detail and the questions each might generate.

PHYSICAL FEATURES

What does it look like, feel like, smell like, sound like? What colour, shape and size is it? What is it made of? Is it a naturally-occurring substance, like bone or stone? Is it made by people, like plastic or glass? Is it made of one substance or several? Is the object complete or do you only have a fragment? Has the object ever been altered or adapted? Has it ever been repaired? Have bits been added or taken away? Is it worn?

The physical features of the object are a good place to start. This is partly because everything else stems from these and partly because all children can answer questions based around their own first-hand experience of the object. All the senses can be used to investigate an object although taste may be inappropriate on grounds both of conservation and hygiene.

Consider whether parts of the object have perished over time; medieval swords usually have the grip missing, for example, and buildings may have lost much of their original paintwork and features because of the elements, changing fashions, deliberate destruction or theft.

CONSTRUCTION

How has the object been made? By hand? By machine? In a mould? In pieces? All at once or over a period of time? By one person or by several people? Has it been glued or glazed or soldered? Has it got rivets, a handle, wires or cogs, a sharp edge or fasteners?

INVESTIGATING AN OBJECT

ASK QUESTIONS ABOUT

PHYSICAL FEATURES — **CONSTRUCTION** — **FUNCTION** — **DESIGN** — **VALUE**

HOW DO WE FIND OUT?

OBSERVATION ▶◀ **RESEARCH/KNOWLEDGE** ▶◀ **DISCUSSION**

CONCLUSIONS

Close observation

Through careful observation of objects it is possible to work out details of their method of construction and manufacture.

This pot shows clear signs of being made by hand. It is uneven and not completely circular. The rounded base is another clue. The decoration has been done by pressing sticks, bones or fingernails into the clay.

The even profile of this jug shows the use of a wheel to shape it. The mottled surface, like orange-peel, is characteristic of salt-glazed pottery. During the course of firing salt is thrown in the kiln, which vapourises and then is deposited on the surface of the pot in the form of a glaze.

This medieval trowel is made from wrought iron. The construction of the handle from thin, twisted strips is characteristic of this method of shaping, which is achieved by heating and hammering the metal.

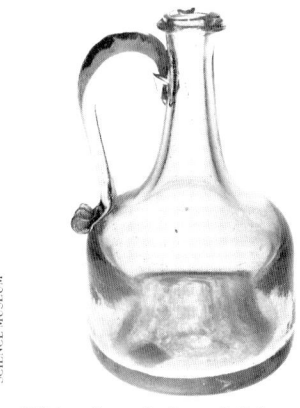

Wheel-made pottery can be recognised by its even appearance and the small horizontal lines running round the pot where the grit in the clay dragged against the potter's hands. The base is generally flat where it was in contact with the wheel.

This glass is hand-blown. The clues are the uneven thickness of the glass and the separate application of the rim and handle. The rim has been cut and not rounded off as it would have been in a mould.

These modern pincers are made from cast iron. The raised trade mark and the lines running down both sides of each handle are signs that a mould was used. The circular section of the handles is achieved through casting rather than hammering and the solidity of the object is another characteristic of the process.

These bottles, showing different stages of production, were made in a mould. The lettering has a soft, rounded appearance common in mould-made products, the general shape of the bottles is regular and in some examples you can see the line where pieces of the mould joined. Sometimes mould marks are smoothed off but it is often possible to feel them even when they can no longer be clearly seen.

FUNCTION

What was the purpose for which the object was made? How has the object been used? Has the use changed?

A coat-hanger reused as a car aerial.

Purpose and use may be two completely different things. In every home or office or classroom, there are objects made for one purpose and used for another; coat-hangers are used as car aerials and jam jars are used as flower vases. Some objects intended to be utilitarian end up as ornaments through deliberate choice or because the object may have become obsolete, out of fashion or rare. Take chamber-pots for instance: these are still being sold in second-hand shops and people buy them to decorate a room or to put plants in, rather than to keep under the bed for an emergency.

You have to look carefully for the clues which tell you both what something's original function was and how it has actually been used. If a teapot has no stains on the inside and is in pristine condition, then it might very well have been valued by its owner simply as a decorative object, or have been rarely used, or have been an unwanted present, or have spent its life stuck in an attic, or it might be new. You would need to find other evidence to confirm one of these theories.

DESIGN

Is the object well designed? Does it do the job it was intended to do efficiently? Were the best materials chosen? Is it aesthetically pleasing? How is it decorated? Why is it decorated?

Only when you have decided what an object was intended to be used for can you assess whether or not it is well designed. A fruit-knife with a silver blade would be useless for cutting steak because silver cannot be honed to a sharp edge. The material has, however, been carefully chosen to avoid tainting the fruit and to look attractive on the table.

Assessing design involves children in making judgements about objects, and they will need to be encouraged to do so in an open-minded way. Something which they think remarkably ugly might nevertheless have been cherished in its day, or by somebody else, as a work of art.

Think also about the constraints on the designer. These include the materials and money available at the time, the level of technology, and the market for which the object was made. A catering-size teapot, for example, is not designed for use by children and the implications of this should be discussed before they decide that it is badly designed because it is too heavy.

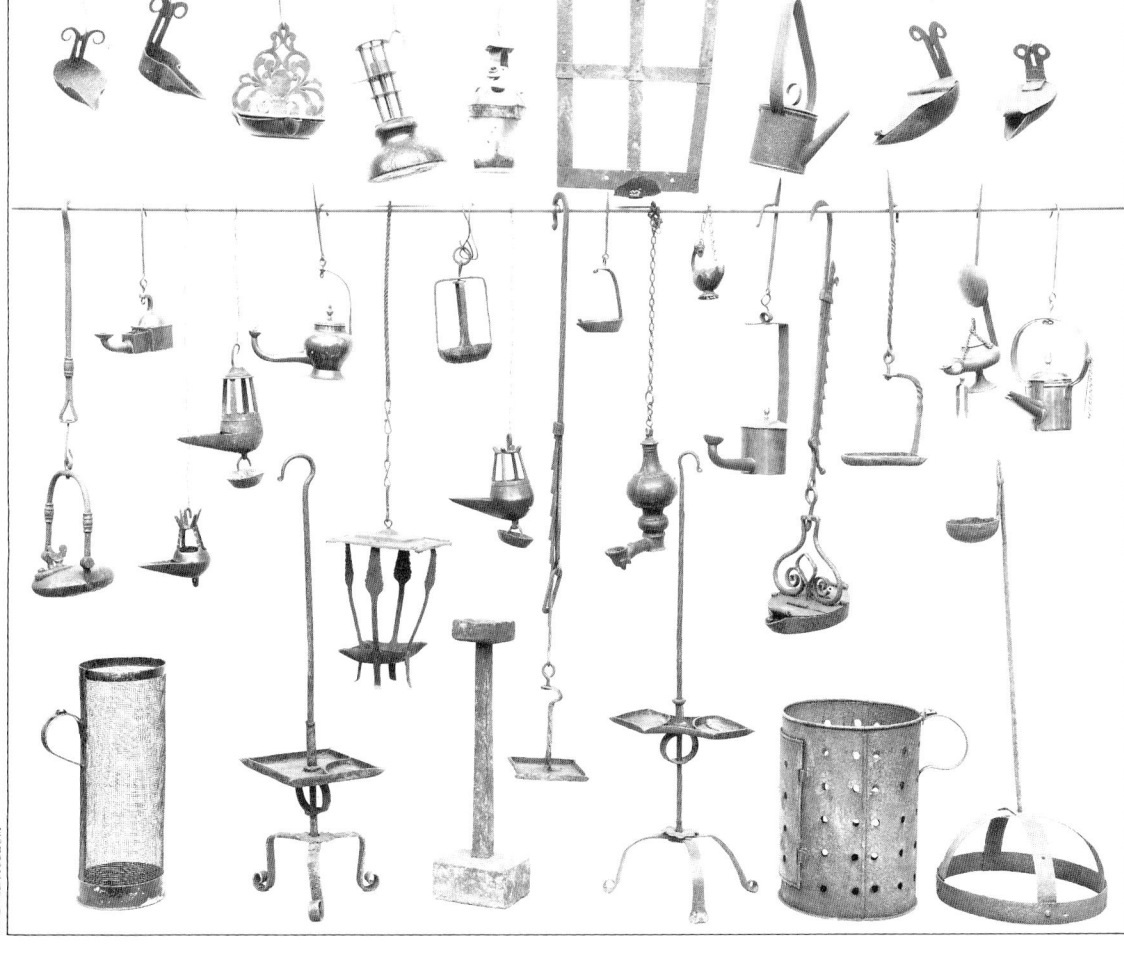

A collection of lamps displaying different design solutions to the problems of supporting a wick, storing fuel, protecting from draught, collecting drips, avoiding smoke marks and adjusting height.

VALUE

What is/was the object worth? In monetary terms? In symbolic terms? In sentimental terms? In social terms? In economic terms? In historical terms?

Value in monetary terms can vary at different times and for different people. An object does not have to be brand new, highly decorated or made of expensive materials to be worth a great deal of money. Objects which are faded, broken or worn can still be expensive. Moreover objects made of materials which are not valued by our society may have been worth a great deal at other times and in other societies.

An object may be worth very little in terms of hard cash but it will be valuable in other ways. To an individual it may have enormous personal value. An object associated with a particular individual may be more widely valued than one whose history is unknown. Artefacts may have religious, political, economic or social significance attached to them, though not everyone will assign the same value to an object; a boat-builder, a wood carver and a nineteenth-century North American Indian would value a dug-out canoe in very different ways.

To try to unravel the significance of an object you need to analyse what it says about the people who made, used and preserved it. What does it reveal about their taste, wealth, status, aspirations, social customs and behaviour, their skills and resources and their economy, technologies, politics and religion?

Types of value

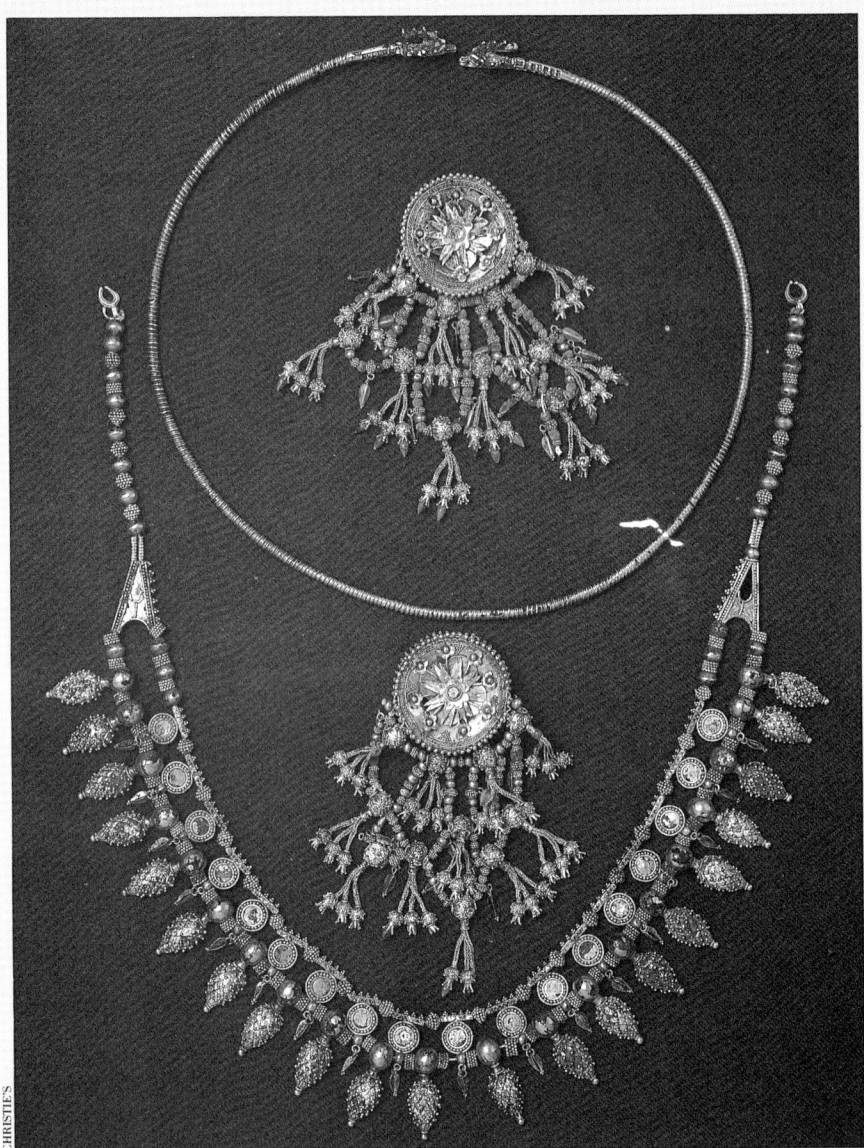

Some materials are thought to have an intrinsic value. Our society values gold. This jewellery combines the value of the gold with the value of rarity. The Scythian necklace sold for £13,000 in 1977. It, the torc and the South Russian gold ear-studs were all made in the fourth century BC.

An auction is sometimes used to settle the current monetary value of an object.

LEARNING FROM OBJECTS

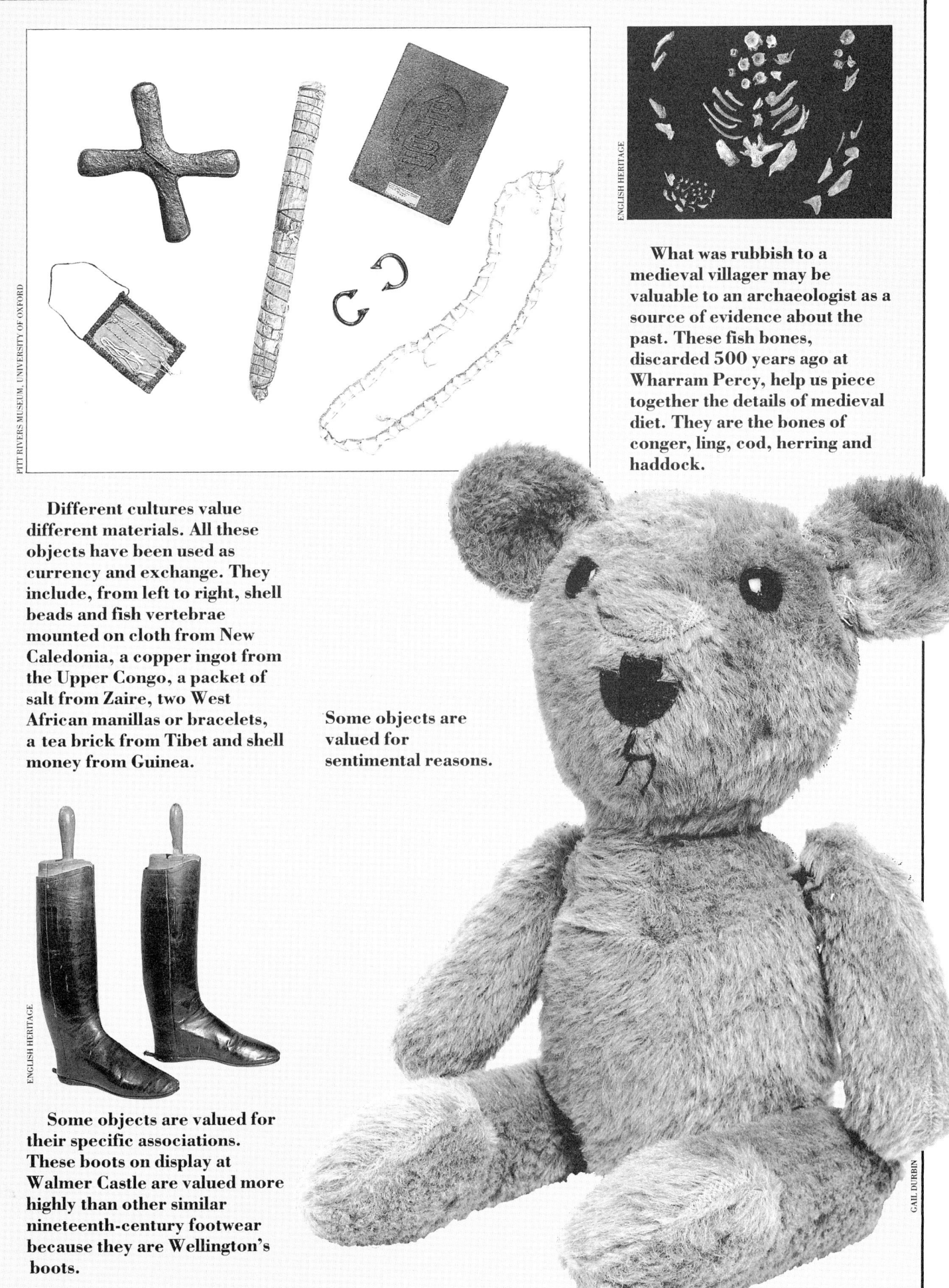

What was rubbish to a medieval villager may be valuable to an archaeologist as a source of evidence about the past. These fish bones, discarded 500 years ago at Wharram Percy, help us piece together the details of medieval diet. They are the bones of conger, ling, cod, herring and haddock.

Different cultures value different materials. All these objects have been used as currency and exchange. They include, from left to right, shell beads and fish vertebrae mounted on cloth from New Caledonia, a copper ingot from the Upper Congo, a packet of salt from Zaire, two West African manillas or bracelets, a tea brick from Tibet and shell money from Guinea.

Some objects are valued for sentimental reasons.

Some objects are valued for their specific associations. These boots on display at Walmer Castle are valued more highly than other similar nineteenth-century footwear because they are Wellington's boots.

11

Initially you may want to give children a worksheet like this to help them analyse an object. Ultimately they should be able to frame their own questions and set about answering them.

Looking at an object

The main things to think about	Some further questions to ask	Things found out through looking	Things to be researched
PHYSICAL FEATURES What does it look and feel like?	What colour is it? What does it smell like? What does it sound like? What is it made of? Is it a natural or manufactured substance? Is the object complete? Has it been altered, adapted, mended? Is it worn?		
CONSTRUCTION How was it made?	Is it handmade or machine-made? Was it made in a mould or in pieces? How has it been fixed together?		
FUNCTION What was it made for?	How has the object been used? Has the use changed?		
DESIGN Is it well designed?	Does it do the job it was intended to do well? Were the best materials used? Is it decorated? How is it decorated? Do you like the way it looks? Would other people like it?		
VALUE What is it worth?	To the people who made it? To the people who used it? To the people who keep it? To you? To a bank? To a museum?		

Not all questions can be answered from observation and the next stage is to go to other sources. Children can use their own previous knowledge and they can ask others; they can use books for research and they can look at other objects for comparison. This may show how typical or atypical an object is, what other solutions people found to a particular set of problems, and the alternative materials available to people working at the same time.

Example of the investigation of an object

Physical features
This teapot feels fairly smooth and is quite light. It is made of porcelain and appears to be complete. It is 17 cms from spout to handle, has a shiny glaze and is decorated in red, blue, green and brown.

Construction
There are two parts to the pot: the lid and the pot itself. Its smooth, even form suggests it was made in a mould although concentric rings on the base suggest that some of the work was done on a wheel. The join between the handle and the body of the pot suggests the handle was made separately and applied later. This may also have been the case with the spout but the evidence is less clear. Some of the decoration is raised which suggests it may have been applied after the glaze.

Function
Previous knowledge tells us this shape is characteristic of a teapot. There is no evidence to suggest it has been used for anything else. If we had never seen a teapot before we could have deduced by the arrangement of the spout and the handle that it was used for pouring something and that the narrowness of the spout suggests a thin liquid. That the liquid may have been hot is suggested by the lid which would keep in the heat, and by the handle which would protect the hand from burning.

Design
Aesthetically the pot may be thought pleasing but this will be a personal response. Some people may like the proportions and find the decoration bold and exciting. Looked at as a functional item, however, the design is curious. Firstly it is very small, much smaller than a modern teapot, and secondly the top of the spout is lower than the top of the pot so that if the pot were filled to the brim liquid would be spilt. This suggests either a design fault or that the pot was not intended to be completely filled.

Value
In monetary terms this pot has a value far in excess of its modern counterpart. Previous knowledge or research may tell us this is an early example of a porcelain teapot and rarity will have added to its financial value. The choice of materials and delicacy of the decoration tell us that this was not bought purely for utility but also for show and we know porcelain to be an expensive commodity in the eighteenth century. That it has survived so long suggests that others have valued it.

We know of no significant personal associations with this teapot nor does it have any sentimental value but it does tell us something about social life and customs in the eighteenth century. The size and the design of the spout suggest that tea was drunk in small quantities in the past. This may have been because it was valuable or it may have been a matter of fashion or it could perhaps have been dangerous in large quantities. Further research would solve this problem. The pot looks expensive and this suggests that tea was drunk in the upper reaches of society. The object itself does not tell us how typical this teapot was in its time.

Exercise
Now attempt a similar analysis of the chair you are sitting on.

USING OBJECTS ACROSS THE CURRICULUM

However you plan to use objects, start by examining them carefully yourself. Read whatever books, teachers' notes or guidebooks are available but be wary of relying too heavily on them. They frequently aim to impart knowledge rather than to help you work things out for yourself through observation.

Sometimes it will be appropriate to work with objects in the classroom and on other occasions you will want to visit sites and museums. Those visits will certainly be more profitable if the skills of object analysis have been taught in the classroom first.

The following examples illustrate a few of the many ways that objects can be used to further curriculum aims and as part of cross-curricular work. They are not intended to be a step by step guide, but rather to illustrate the range of applications.

We have not linked these ideas to specific subjects and attainment targets in the National Curriculum, partly because the details of all foundation subjects have yet to be published, and also because you will want to determine your own focus, depending both on whether you are a primary teacher or a subject specialist in a secondary school, and also on the needs of your pupils. Each example can be adapted for different age ranges or to serve the needs of different areas of the curriculum. The abbey visit could, for example, concentrate on Attainment Target 8: Measures or Attainment Target 12: Handling Data in the Maths curriculum; it could deal with Attainment Target 1: Speaking and Listening in the English curriculum, or it could further an understanding of evidence in the History curriculum. In Science, Attainment Target 6: Types and Uses of Materials and Attainment Target 9: Earth and Atmosphere have particular relevance to site visits, and the Technology curriculum makes constant reference to drawing examples from other times and cultures.

Topic: Abbeys

Binham Priory.

Equipment/site visit: Site visit to abbey where the remains include the footings of the abbey, cloister and some of the abbey buildings.

Purpose of activity: To learn about the layout of an abbey and what can be discovered from building remains.

Method: At the site draw a measured plan of the abbey buildings using triangulation, a measuring tape or an arbitrary scale. The pupils discuss the relative size of the buildings, shape of spaces, nearness to water, etc. They are given cards with the names of the buildings that might be found in such an abbey, eg. church, cloister, infirmary (or hospital), and chapter house (or meeting room). They discuss the function of each of these areas and the evidence that might remain and then they have to try to put these names to the buildings they have just mapped. Discuss whether the choices are reasonable, and what other evidence they might need to confirm these conclusions. Mark building names on the measured plan. Back at school compare with the standard plan for an abbey of that order.

One of the benefits of this method is that pupils are pleased to discover how much they can work out about life in an abbey for themselves rather than from books or their teacher. They are also surprised to find how much can be learnt from apparently minimal remains.

Topic: Childcare

The nursery in an Edwardian doll's house, with some later additions.

Equipment/site visit: Pupils make a visit to a local social history museum to examine examples of babies' clothing, portraits, toys and feeding equipment.

Purpose of activity: To show through the objects how attitudes to childcare have changed.

Method: The pupils examine items and are constantly encouraged to compare what they see with what they know to be used today, eg. elaborate dresses with stretch nylon romper suits; buttons and pins for fastening, with press studs and stretch fabrics; pottery feeding bottles which have inaccessible tubes with plastic bottles and throw-away teats that can be boiled. Pupils draw what they see and annotate drawings to show detail and bring out comparisons with the present. Discuss findings.

Pupils are often aware there are differences between daily life and healthcare in Victorian England and today but rarely appreciate how great these were. The use of objects brings home the contrasts in a graphic manner. Later work might relate some of their observations to infant mortality levels.

Topic: Textiles

Eighteenth-century embroidered chair back from Marble Hill House.

Equipment: Visit to a historic house.

Purpose of visit: To study the wall-hangings and soft furnishings in a historic house and to use them as a stimulus for design.

Method: Take pupils on a tour of a historic house, noting the rooms which have examples of soft furnishings and wall-hangings. Discuss with the pupils how appropriate the designs/fabrics are for the rooms they are in.

Set the pupils the following problem and give them time to make a more detailed study of one of the rooms to help them work on it. The owner of the house wishes to commission a set of wall-hangings for the shop. The pupils have to submit a set of designs for these together with details of cost, fabrics, methods of construction and advice on conservation and display. They should also submit a sample of the kind of hanging they have designed. The prime purpose of these wall-hangings is to make the shop look more attractive and, though the designs and fabrics used can be contemporary ones, they should in some way reflect the furnishings of the house.

Many designers use historical examples to inspire their work. Pupils can do this as well. This approach shows that it is legitimate and productive to use objects to stimulate fresh creative work.

Topic: Castles

Working out the height of the castle motte at Carisbrooke.

Equipment: A castle with most of the outer defences in place.

Purpose of activity: To find out about methods of attack and defence in the medieval period through observation.

Method: Ask pupils how they can tell that castles were built to stop people getting into them. At the site tell pupils they are soldiers in the army of someone who wishes to attack the castle; they have been sent to spy on it and to bring back information to help plan the attack. They have to think up a suitable disguise which will get them past the sentries, and then make their way round the perimeter and then to the centre of the castle, noting all the obstacles which they will have to overcome when they attack it. They have then to prepare their report. Back at school compare each group's report. Did they make a note of all the places where the defenders could mount archers? Did they miss any vital clues? Most pupils can generalise about the defensive role of a castle but it is not until they have actually seen the thickness of the walls and the successive lines of defence that they really internalise this information.

Topic: Light

Bull's eye lantern.

Equipment: As many examples as possible of such things as candlesticks, oil-lamps, rush-lights, storm-lanterns, torches, table-lamps, and the candles, oil, batteries and so on which make them work. Work in a room (such as a science laboratory if possible) where naked flames can be controlled, and black-out obtained.

Purpose of activity: To examine the advantages and disadvantages of creating light through different means.

Method: This is an exciting and dramatic approach which allows pupils to experience for themselves the difficulties involved in creating and maintaining light.

In a darkened room, examine the sort of light created by each piece of equipment and describe the possible uses of the light: inside only, inside or outside, for a large room, for individual use, for static use or for use on the move. Pupils could devise experiments for comparing the lights.

Now examine the power supply for each of the lights – chemical, combination of oil or wax and so on. What are the advantages and disadvantages of each?

Topic: The Royal family

Commemorative jug and plate for the coronation of George VI in 1937. Circular tray proposed as a souvenir of the coronation of Edward VIII.

Equipment: Items bearing as wide a variety as possible of royal pictures, symbols or insignia, eg. coins, commemorative mugs, product labels with the royal seal 'By Appointment', or postcards. These could be either brought into school or studied in a museum or historic house.

Purpose of activity: To examine the imagery used by royalty, and to see how this imagery is used to communicate with subjects.

Method: Pupils first conduct a survey of the images they have found. They should make a list of all the different types they have, such as Latin mottoes, stylised likenesses, actual likenesses, and emblems, and where these occur. They can then examine the message being given in each case. Is it very formal, in a code only a few will understand, claiming special powers or sovereignty? In each case, eg. jam pot, letterhead or coin, who would be expected to see and understand it? They could discuss whether there was any clear relationship between the image and where it was used.

A further level of study would be to research which other individuals or organisations produce similar mottoes, logos or slogans for publicity purposes, and to examine where these occur, for example, in municipal arms, on lamp posts, school mottoes, badges or album sleeves.

Symbolism is a difficult concept to tackle with children. By using examples found in all their homes they can see it in use and begin to grasp this abstract concept.

Topic: Prehistory

Barbed and tanged arrowheads.

Equipment: Box of flint tools (from a loan service), eg. chipped hand axe, polished axe, arrowhead, borer, scraper, hammerstone.

Purpose of activity: To learn as much as possible about prehistoric life from the tools people left behind and to assess the value of archaeological evidence.

Method: Pupils work in groups, each with a flint tool. They are asked to examine it carefully, and to generate some questions such as: How was it made? Does the tool have an edge? How has the edge been made? Can the item be held comfortably? Does this suggest how it might have been used? Would it be easier to use with a handle? How could the handle be fixed? What tasks could have been performed with the tool? What skills were needed to make and use it?

The pupils draw the tool and record their findings. Items are passed round and the exercise repeated until all items have been seen. The pupils attempt to answer their own questions.

The activity ends with a general discussion of what these tools demonstrate about prehistoric life, such as the limitations of the materials available, the sophisticated treatment of those materials, the time taken to do specific jobs with them and reflections on the organisation of the society that used them. The pupils discuss why certain materials survive, what materials might be missing and the other kinds of evidence that might be available.

Topic: *A Christmas Carol* by Charles Dickens

Magic lantern slide.

Equipment: A museum loan collection or museum display of Victorian children's toys, eg. magic lantern, china doll, rocking-horse, train set, doll's house.

Purpose of activity. To examine the way Charles Dickens uses descriptions of objects to create images and atmosphere.

Method: Read to the class the description of the well-to-do Christmas (First Spirit) and then of the Cratchit's Christmas (Second Spirit) in *A Christmas Carol*. Examine the toys and see which Christmas they belong to; talk about who would probably play with them – boys, girls, individuals or groups; are they games for the body or for the brain? Discuss with pupils why they think these things were kept safe and preserved so that they still exist today. Why can't they see the toys of poor children? Talk about the most fashionable toys today, the favourites of individual children, and whether they still take care of the toys that they no longer play with.

Then go back to *A Christmas Carol* and see how Dickens uses descriptions of objects and locations to create the effect he wants, for instance in the description of Scrooge's dwelling, the shops or the town. Older pupils might then compare Dickens' work with other writers, eg. Charlotte Brontë, where strong images are created with little reference to physical things.

Topic: The role of women

Laundry equipment.

Topic: The Second World War

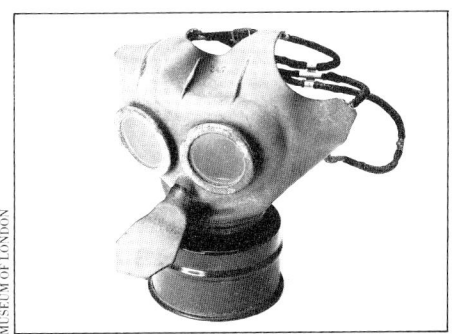

Second World War gas mask.

Topic: The school building

Westbury Centre, Barking.

Equipment: A collection of domestic items from a museum loan service including nineteenth-century mechanical food chopper, 1920s carpet cleaner, series of old irons, a wash dolly and dolly tub.

Purpose of lesson: To discover whether the introduction of modern technology in the home has been labour-saving or time-saving and how it might have influenced the lives of women. To use artefacts as a source of information.

Method: The pupils examine objects carefully to work out how things were powered and used and then discuss their findings. They then design a programme of one or more experiments to discover whether new technology is labour-saving or time-saving. If the owner of the objects allows them to be used, pupils might compare the time taken to wash an item in a dolly tub with the time taken using a machine. After using one of these objects initial enthusiasm gives way to tiredness and boredom and a corresponding understanding of how arduous housework was in the past. Pupils might also search contemporary accounts for information about the length of time devoted to doing the washing, and its frequency, in the past. They present their findings in report form then move on to a discussion of whether women today have more time to do other things, and what their findings might contribute to a debate on whether a woman's place is in the home.

Equipment: Ask pupils to bring in anything they can find associated with life on the home front, and make your own collection from junk shops, relatives, etc. Try to get such things as a gas mask, ration books, shrapnel, photographs or uniform. Your local museum might provide a loan box.

Purpose of activity: To find out about life on the Home Front from physical remains.

Method: Divide the objects into those associated with civilians and with soldiers. How many tell you about the lives of both? Look at all the artefacts. What can they tell you about life in the war? Many pupils' ideas about war are culled from Hollywood and fiction and fantasy. Contact with these objects helps to bring home how war affected ordinary people's lives. Ask the pupils to draw up an evidence chart showing what they can say for certain about the period 1939-45 from looking at the artefacts, what they think they can say about it, and what questions the objects have raised. Ask them to think about how they might set about answering those questions. Can they think of other types of artefacts which might help them? What kinds of things will the artefacts not tell them and what other sources will they need?

Equipment: The school itself, clipboards, paper, pencils.

Purpose of lesson: To see what can be learnt about the history of the school from its buildings.

Method: Tell the group that they are going to search the school for clues about its history. Discuss with the group the kinds of evidence which they might find and then take them on a tour of the school. They should look for such things as old gas-fittings, extensions or repairs to the exterior, a date over the school door, the arrangement of the rooms, old signs ('boys' and 'girls' entrances), honours boards, graffiti on the desks, obsolete equipment, rotting wood, flat roofs on 1960s buildings. Pupils are surprised to find how much they have failed to 'see' in a very familiar building. They are also pleased to discover the number of clues to life in the past that can be found in their immediate environment.

Afterwards discuss with the group what they have learnt and ask them to compile a list of the questions that have been raised by their tour of the school. They can then plan the necessary research.

DEVELOPING SKILLS FOR WORKING WITH OBJECTS

The best way to develop skills is to need them and to use them in real situations, refining them with practice. When using objects in the classroom the development of skills such as observation, deduction, language and recording will go hand-in-hand with the study of the object. If you are making a visit, however, time may be short and the level of excitement or the diversions such that the skills will need to have been prepared in advance of the confrontation with the real Norman castle, gallery of Roman cooking equipment or early motor car, in order to get the most from the experience.

Relating to objects may come more easily to some than others (and not always to those perceived by teachers to be the 'brightest') but you cannot assume it is an innate ability and, just like reading and map-work, it has to be taught. Learning from objects takes time and practice.

The following are a series of exercises that will help to develop some of the necessary skills. Inevitably, no single skill is taught in isolation, and the activities are grouped only roughly. The exercises have been largely designed as games to make the activity fun and to drive the learning home. You don't need museum objects to be able to do them. When at a site, you may find it useful to refer back to these activities to remind pupils of the skills and approach they should be employing.

LEARNING TO LOOK

When we look at something we do not always 'see' it or learn from it. Visual skills are not simply the ability to convert what we see into an acceptable drawing or a work of art. They enable us to observe and understand and judge what we see and to elicit ideas and information from non-verbal sources.

Our visual skills are often placed low in the hierarchy after skills of literacy and numeracy. In school one of the dangers of taking a narrow view of visual skills is that they come to be seen as the preserve of the specialist art teacher. There are seldom specialist art teachers in the primary school, and in the secondary classroom, outside art lessons, drawing is often relegated to a time-filling, space-filling activity after the 'real' work has been done. This is a pity.

Learning to see is a sophisticated skill that requires conscious effort to develop. You need to slow up, to take time to study. A cursory glance may tell only half the story whereas a conscious, thoughtful study may provide clues that were not at first apparent. Any activity that encourages you to engage closely with an object will heighten your powers of observation.

A magnifying glass, a card frame or a cheap dental mirror can all encourage children to look more closely at objects.

DEVELOPING SKILLS

String Map We often fail to observe things carefully because we think we already know about them. To bring this point home to older pupils give them a long piece of string. Knot the ends. Their task is now to form the string into an outline of England, Scotland and Wales. There is likely to be a confident start followed by much uncertainty. Once the task is complete compare the results with an atlas and look in particular at proportion and the relationship of different parts of the country. Underline the point that when recording we need always to be referring back to the real thing as our visual memory may not be as reliable as we imagine.

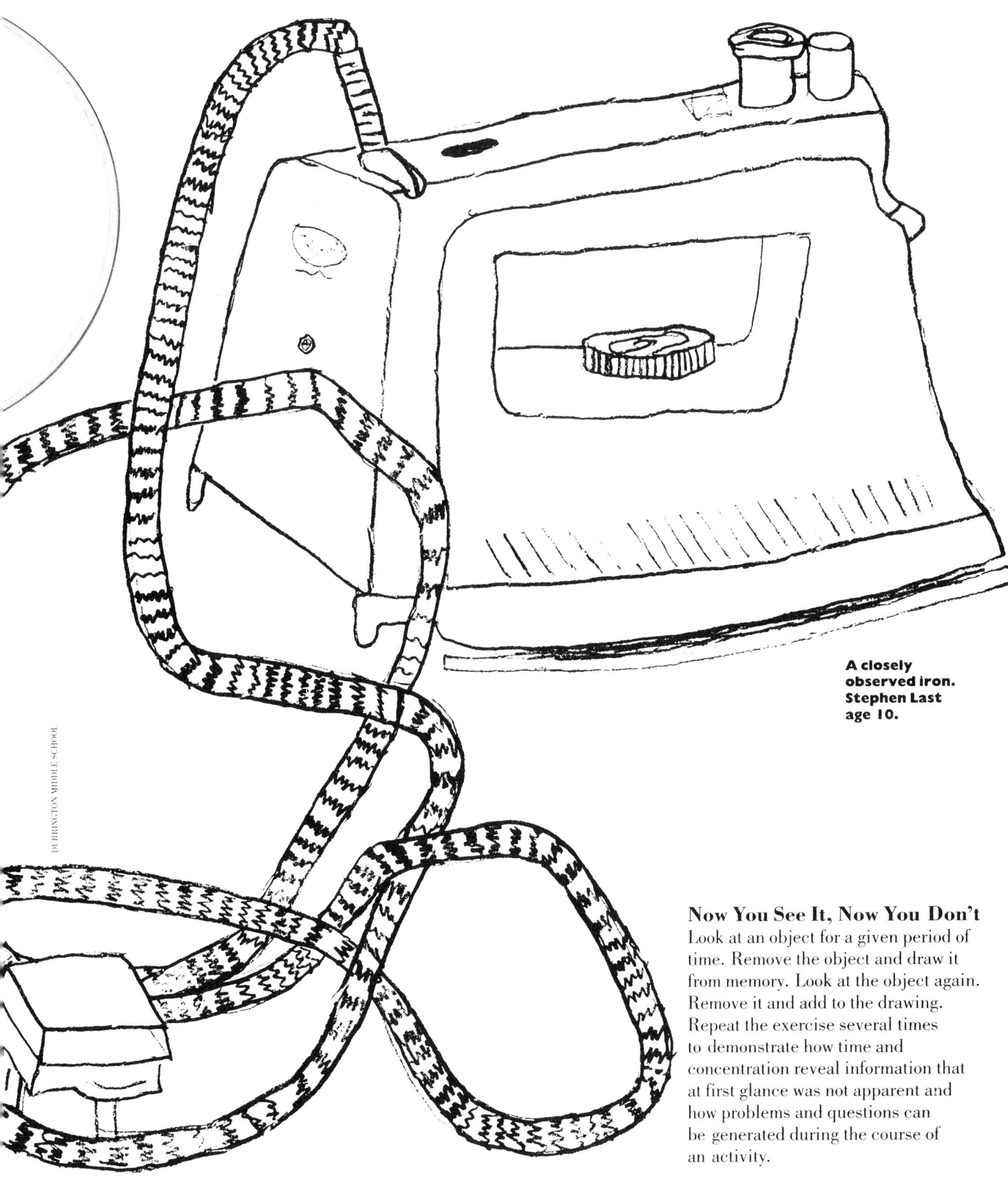

A closely observed iron. Stephen Last age 10.

Now You See It, Now You Don't Look at an object for a given period of time. Remove the object and draw it from memory. Look at the object again. Remove it and add to the drawing. Repeat the exercise several times to demonstrate how time and concentration reveal information that at first glance was not apparent and how problems and questions can be generated during the course of an activity.

19

LEARNING TO DESCRIBE

Describing artefacts both requires and encourages the development of a broad vocabulary.

Feely Bags Put objects in cloth draw-string bags. Allow pupils to feel the objects and ask them to describe them. If the objects are unfamiliar or difficult to identify this should force pupils to use a range of vocabulary to describe them. Alternatively the activity can be adapted as a drawing exercise. Instead of describing the object pupils have to draw them from their feel.

The Case of the Confused Card Index One object is put out for every pupil. Each pupil writes a catalogue card for their object. Each reads out his or her card in turn, omitting the name of the object, and the rest of the group match the card with the object. This may be a useful exercise for pupils developing their own classroom museum. They will need to keep good records just as a curator would.

LEARNING TO RECORD

Drawing is one of the best ways to learn about an object and record it. The aesthetic quality of the drawing is unimportant provided the activity keeps the eye and the mind engaged and allows time to consider texture, shape, and function. Indeed it is important to make the distinction between drawing for recording purposes and drawing for art, in the same way that you would teach pupils to distinguish the appropriate language and form for an official letter or a poem. We can all draw if our confidence has not been undermined in childhood and we can certainly all record through drawing.

Encourage children to give an indication of size by adding scales or measurement to their drawings. Lack of confidence in putting a line on a page can lead to children never getting any drawing done and simply wearing a hole in the page by constant rubbing out. Consider the following strategies: ban rubbers to force children to commit themselves; or suggest the use of rubbers only when the fresh line has been correctly placed; or issue wax crayons or coloured pencils so that

careful planning becomes essential. Encourage pupils to look carefully when drawing by choosing a familiar object but setting it at an unfamiliar angle, eg. a bicycle upside down, resting on its handlebars, or a classroom chair on its side.

DEVELOPING SKILLS

A familiar object drawn from an unfamiliar angle.

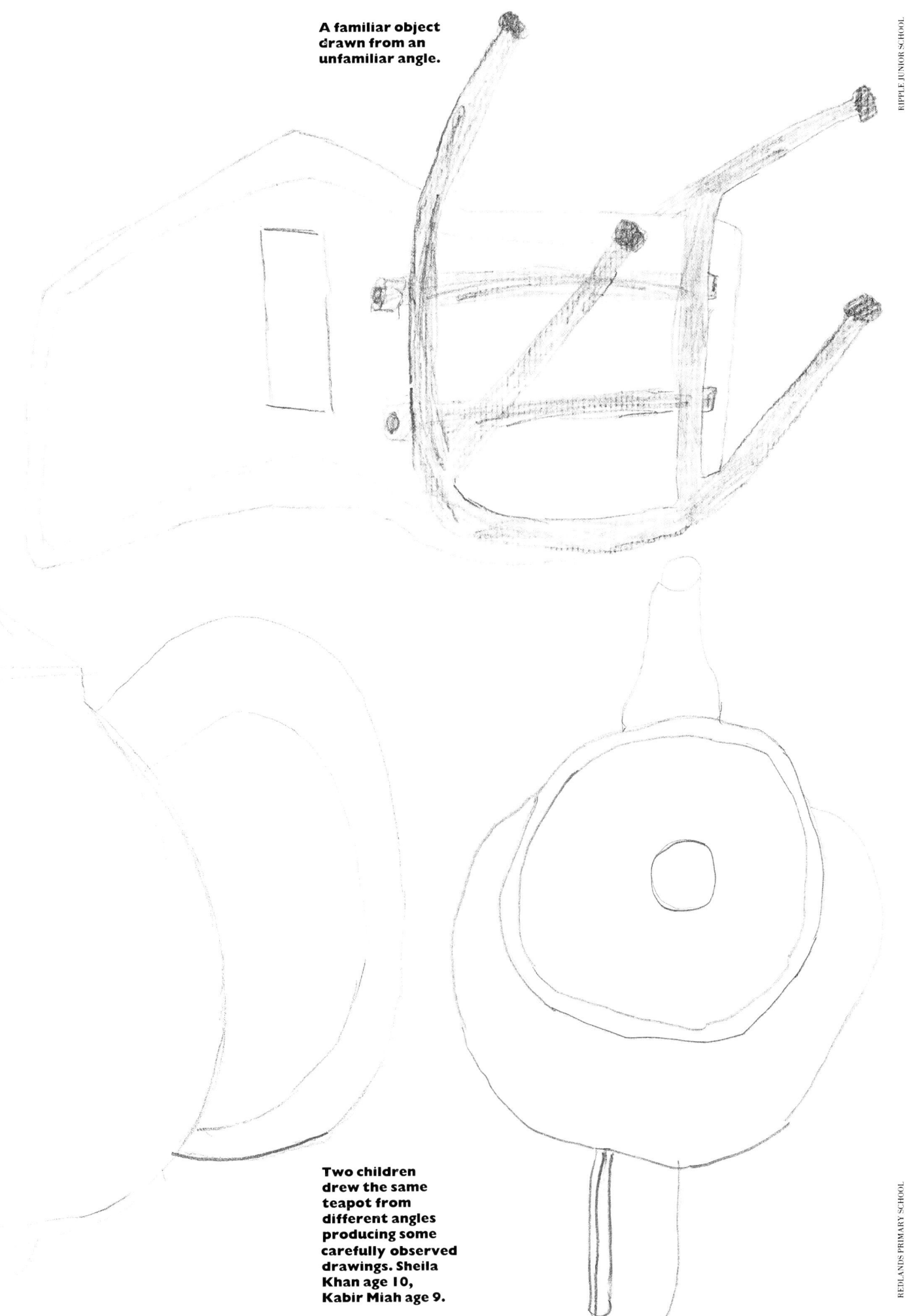

Two children drew the same teapot from different angles producing some carefully observed drawings. Sheila Khan age 10, Kabir Miah age 9.

DEVELOPING SKILLS

If you want pupils to make written records of what they see make sure they know what kind of writing is required. Depending on the situation some forms are better than others. Full sentences are probably not required on site, when labelled drawings or note form may be most appropriate. Lack of precision often mars written descriptions. Stress the need to record the detail which may provide important clues; it is not enough just to name something. If you want to free children from carrying clipboards, paper and pencils at a site then small hand-held tape-recorders offer an alternative method of recording that may also motivate the less literate pupil. In some of the following activities a tape-recorder could be substituted where a written record is needed.

Sewing-Machine Game Ask pupils to draw a sewing-machine from memory. All are likely to start confidently but check how many of the finished machines would work. Now draw a sewing-machine from observation. Check the effectiveness of the machines again. This should demonstrate to pupils the importance of careful observation and also how drawing an item may be a means of understanding it. You could try using an iron or a washing-machine or a bicycle or a tin-opener or a piece of equipment that everyone uses in school.

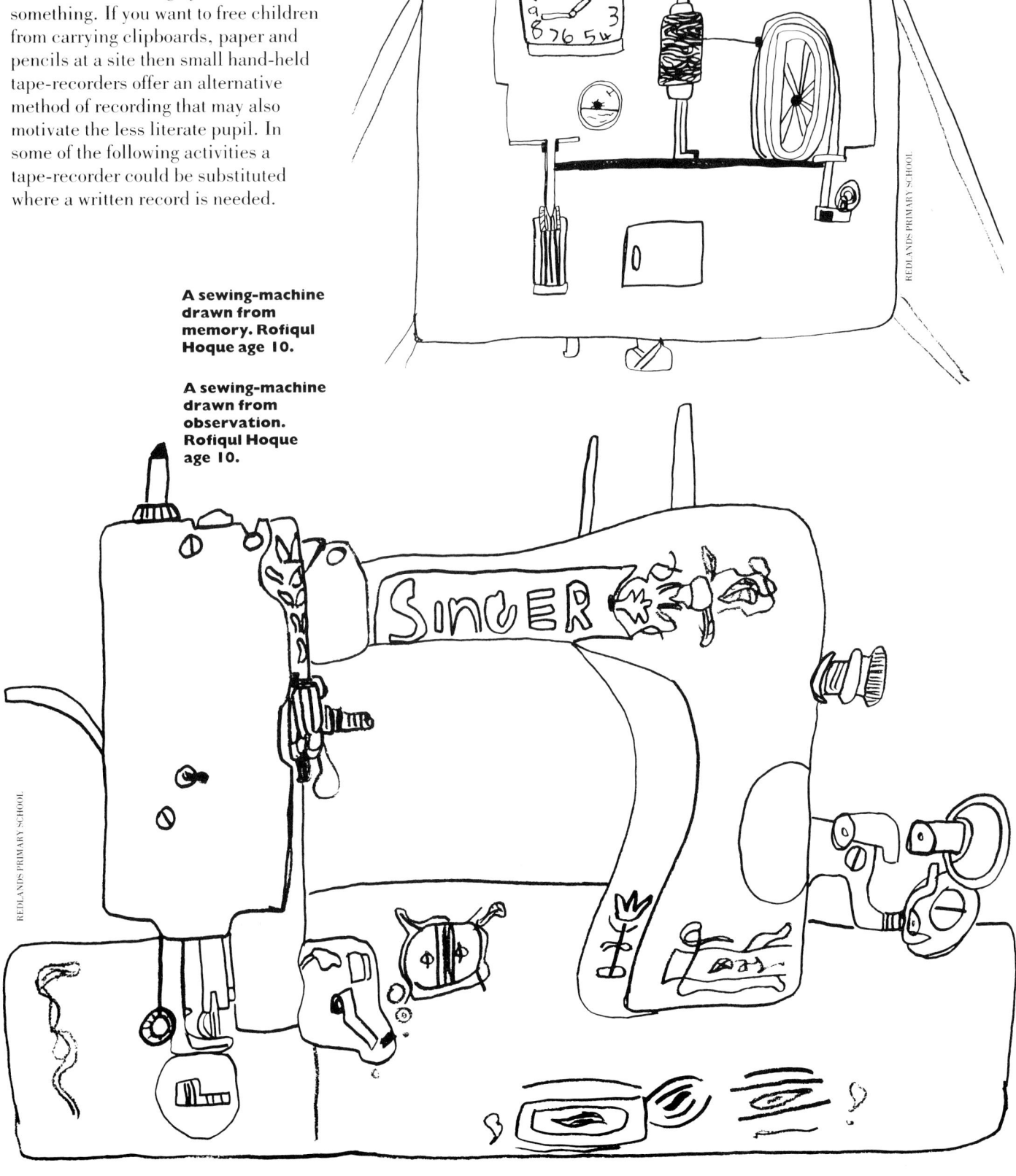

A sewing-machine drawn from memory. Rofiqul Hoque age 10.

A sewing-machine drawn from observation. Rofiqul Hoque age 10.

Giant Drawing To help get away from minute drawings in the centre of a page, provide something very small to be drawn very large, eg. a matchbox to cover a whole sheet of sugar paper. Provision of thick felt-tip pens or wax crayons might help. Discuss the significance of scale; detail can more easily be shown on a large drawing but a drawing can become misleading if there has been a considerable change of scale.

The Yellow Crayon Game Pupils work in groups of about five. Each is given a yellow crayon and asked to write a description of it. The group's crayons are then mixed together and the descriptions read out in turn and an attempt made to fit the descriptions to the right crayon. This helps to underline the importance of careful observation reflected in precise descriptive vocabulary. Depending on the ability of the participants, it may be necessary to use several brands of crayon. You could substitute rulers.

Blind Drawing Pupils work in pairs. Each has an object that cannot be seen by their partner. They each write a description of their object. Descriptions are swapped and each pupil does a drawing of the object based on the description. The activity can end here with a discussion of the resulting drawings and comparison with the object. Alternatively, other objects could be introduced and the exercise repeated in the light of experience. To learn the importance of redrafting their work pupils could examine their partner's drawings and, without revealing the object, they could rewrite their description in order to help their partner reproduce the object more accurately.

Martian Down Your Way Children work in pairs. One child has an everyday object, eg. a chair, a pencil case or a book. The other child is a Martian radio interviewer who records an interview with the earth dweller about the object so that back on Mars the listeners can learn more about the new-found planet Earth. With practice this activity will develop vocabulary and provide an opportunity for imaginative interpretation.

The yellow crayon

The yellow pencil in front of me is a Stadtler. It has a slanting edge on the lead. It's been sharpened. It's left a frilly edge. If you put the pencil so Stadtler is up the right way it will have nine arrows on the right and three on the left. It also has someone's initials on it and by that it has a few dents.
David Francis age 9

I've got a yellow pencil in front of me. On the side it says BRAZIL 000 MULTICOLOR 000 Faber-Castell. At the end it is dirty with little holes and a dent next to the side and bits of paint coming off at the end of the pencil. It has a black piece of paint on the middle of the pencil. It has a blob of dirt under the R in MULTICOLOR and a black dot on top of C and O in MULTICOLOR. It hasn't a very even edge where it's been sharpened. It has a clean wooden end there. It's been sharpened. It has a slant end which you write with. Half the side has wood on it and the rest is just crayon.
Daioni Banks age 9

I have a pale yellow pencil in front of me. It has silver writing on it. There are quite a lot of chips out of the bottom of it. There is a long point and it is sloped and has rings round it. At the top there is a wavy line where it has been sharpened. It has a few black dots on it.
Anthony Brackston age 9

The crayon is yellow and blunt. At the colouring end there is an ink mark. At the other end there is a black and red mark. There are no symbols or writing on the crayon. It is a hexagon shape and has a few teeth marks. At the end where it has been sharpened there is a wavy line.
Richard Terrington age 9

This yellow pencil has one blunt end and one end is sharpened. Both ends have wavy lines where it's been sharpened. It is made in Great Britain. At one end of the pencil the next time it's sharpened it will sharpen a number 5 out. There is a dent by the Great Britain. It has a silver writing on it. It has a blue mark. There is a little picture and it is half scraped off.
Russell Galvin age 9

A hand-held tape-recorder.

LEARNING TO ASK QUESTIONS

Pupils will be helped to work independently from objects if they can formulate questions about them. They need to get beyond 'What is it?' and 'How old is it?' so that they can produce more questions spontaneously. Try the following:

The Back-to-Back Game Pupils work in pairs sitting back to back. Pupil A is given an object but only offers information about it in response to questions asked by pupil B who has ten or twenty questions to find out what it is. A may not name the object. This is a demanding exercise because in order to succeed the questions have to be asked in a structured way, eg. 'Is it heavy?', 'How heavy is it?', 'Tell me what it weighs'. It will not work if the object is unfamiliar to the pupil. Children will learn that the information obtained depends on the phrasing of the question. Follow up by discussing what types of questions provide useful answers.

Big Mac Ask your pupils to work through the 50 activities. Alternatively you might bring in some hamburger boxes and get them to formulate similar questions. Go through the list of questions and divide them into those that can be answered from the box itself and those that require further knowledge or research.

Discuss the value of dealing first with the questions that can be answered by the object before moving on to those that require further research. Discuss the range of information and ideas that can be acquired from an everyday object.

Lego Two pupils construct a random shape from a few pieces of Lego and keep their model concealed. The remaining pupils have an identical set of Lego and their task is to make an identical construction. As they may not look at the model, they can only find out what their construction should look like by asking the two pupils questions. These two may not provide any information except in response to a direct question. The importance of framing questions precisely soon becomes apparent.

LEARNING TO CLASSIFY

Well-developed powers of observation and the ability to learn from objects depend on identifying and classifying the type of information an object yields: colour, texture, shape, smell, sound, weight, materials, design, structure, function, value will all be revealed. The following activities are intended to help children learn to classify what can be discovered.

The No-Name Game The pupils work in teams. Team *A* chooses a familiar object, eg. a chair, which they keep secret. They then take it in turns to tell team *B* something about it. The aim of the game is to say five or ten accurate things about the object without team *B* guessing what it is. The teams then swap roles. Pupils soon learn that there is more to be said about an object than its name and function.

50 ways to look at a Big Mac box

A Big Mac box.

1. Smell it.
2. Taste it.
3. Feel it all over.
4. Does it make a noise?
5. What are its measurements? Height, weight, diameter?
6. Describe its shape, colour and any decoration.
7. Can you write a description of it that would give a clear picture to someone who has never seen a Big Mac box? (A sketch would help.)
8. Why is it the size it is?
9. Are all McDonald's boxes the same size?
10. Have the sizes of McDonald's boxes changed over the years; have they changed with metrification?
11. How much has the box's shape been determined by the material used, the method of construction and the box's function?
12. Why isn't the box plain white (or black, or purple)?
13. What is the function of the decoration?
14. What does the lettering tell you?
15. Why are symbols, logos and trade marks so important in our society?
16. How much is the name 'Big Mac' a reflection of the fashions of our time?

Kim's Game I Put twenty objects on a tray. Allow pupils to look at them for a given period. Cover or remove objects. Pupils recall as many objects as possible. This depends simply on memory but...

Kim's Game II ...instead of asking pupils to recall the names of things ask for certain categories of information, eg. items made from wood, things a parent would use, tools, things made from animal products. Alternatively you could ask the pupils to provide the categories themselves.

The Museum Game Give pupils about six disparate objects and ask them to imagine they are curators and have to organise these objects in one case. Would they choose themes such as materials or methods of manufacture or would they display them for their aesthetic qualities? This could be turned into an exercise on chronology if the objects were of similar function but different dates. This exercise should demonstrate how a number of different lines of study are suggested by one set of objects.

LEARNING TO RELATE STRUCTURE TO FUNCTION

The design of most artefacts is influenced principally by the use to which they will be put. Other influences are the aesthetic judgement of the designer, economic considerations and the availability and appropriateness of materials from which to make them. Current tastes and preferences also have an influence. Children need to understand these fundamental points in order to be able to move to the higher levels of thought about objects.

Horses for Courses Before children can be critical about a maker's choice of materials they need to distinguish and name different materials. Make a classroom collection of examples, eg. brass, iron, pottery, wax, wood, lead, marble, chalk, or ask the children to assemble one. Discuss the different characteristics of each material. You could experiment with them and test them for water resistance, hardness, conductivity, strength or weight. Discuss what each material might most efficiently be used for and then discuss the problems of finding suitable materials to perform specific tasks. This activity teaches an understanding of the characteristics of different materials.

---

17. What does the circled R signify?
18. What material was used to make the box?
19. What raw material was used to produce this material?
20. Is this a renewable resource?
21. What does this say about attitudes towards conservation in our society?
22. Why was this particular material chosen?
23. What are its advantages; its disadvantages?
24. How might the box have been different if a different material had been used, for example, wood, or ceramics, or metal, or paper?
25. What can you learn from looking at the box and the lettering about how the box was made?
26. At what stage of manufacture do you think the lettering was applied?
27. Have you ever seen anything like this being made? What does that suggest to you about our society?
28. Is the box well designed?
29. Does it work well for the purposes for which it was designed?
30. How might the design be improved?

31. If someone twenty, fifty or one hundred years ago had set about designing a container for a hamburger, how might they have done it differently?
32. Did people eat hamburgers then?
33. What might the hamburger container of the future be like?
34. What does the number on the inside bottom of the box signify?
35. Is this a clue as to where the box was made?
36. Where was the box made?
37. What did these boxes replace?
38. Why not just serve a hamburger on a plate?
39. What does a Big Mac box tell us about the people who use it, the people who pass it out and our society in general?
40. Show the Big Mac box to as many people as you can within a ten-minute period. How many people failed to recognize the box? What does this tell you?
41. Would you get this response in Birmingham, Aberystwyth, Glasgow, Sutton, Exeter or Paris? What does this tell you?
42. Where is the headquarters of McDonald's? What does this tell you?

43. Do you deserve a break today?
44. How many of these boxes are used across Britain every day?
45. For how long is each box actually used?
46. What is done with them after they have been used?
47. Why do you find Big Mac boxes on pavements, in parks and on beaches?
48. Is there anything that could be done to recycle these boxes?
49. Is there anything that could replace them?
50. What do you think is the single most significant thing about a Big Mac box? Why?

And now, imagine that you are a Big Mac box and write the story of your life.

What's It For? Make a collection of similar artefacts where the function is not necessarily known, for example, tongs (eyebrow tweezers, fire tongs, sugar tongs, sardine or other food-serving tongs, old wooden washing tongs, ice tongs) or brushes (hair, dog, teeth, wool-cards, hearth, bottle). Try to work out what each one was used for. Discuss the different materials used and why they have been chosen. Discuss the nature of the choices facing a maker.

The Conservation Game This activity shows how some materials are more suitable for certain functions than others. It also illustrates the problems of conservation faced by museums and why some objects should not be handled. Make a collection of different materials, for example an eggshell, a piece of new white cloth, a piece of glazed cotton, a piece of white paper or coloured sugar paper, a piece of clear plastic, a glossy photograph. Divide each thing in half and put one half in a safe place. Without explaining why you are doing it, pass the other halves round the class from hand to hand three times. Compare the two halves. What changes have occurred? Discuss how you might choose the material of something that was to be handled frequently. Might the class have handled things differently if they had been told to take care of them? Discuss the implications of your findings for museums that are trying to preserve objects for hundreds of years or to historians or archaeologists who are assessing evidence. The activity could be varied by burying objects to discover the consequences of damp or by leaving items exposed to the light.

LEARNING TO FORMULATE AND TEST HYPOTHESES

When children are first asked to work with objects they have a tendency to guess at an answer and stick with it no matter what. Working in a group discussing an object one young child will say 'It's a coat-hanger', another will say 'It's a spanner', and then they simply repeat themselves and get no further. Children may also come to a full stop with the answer 'I don't know'. They need to learn ways of going beyond this by using the evidence available to them.

Mystery Object Give pupils a mystery object and make a chart with the following headings.

Each fact or idea should be recorded separately on the chart. Children could perhaps be asked to prepare a final report with their conclusions.

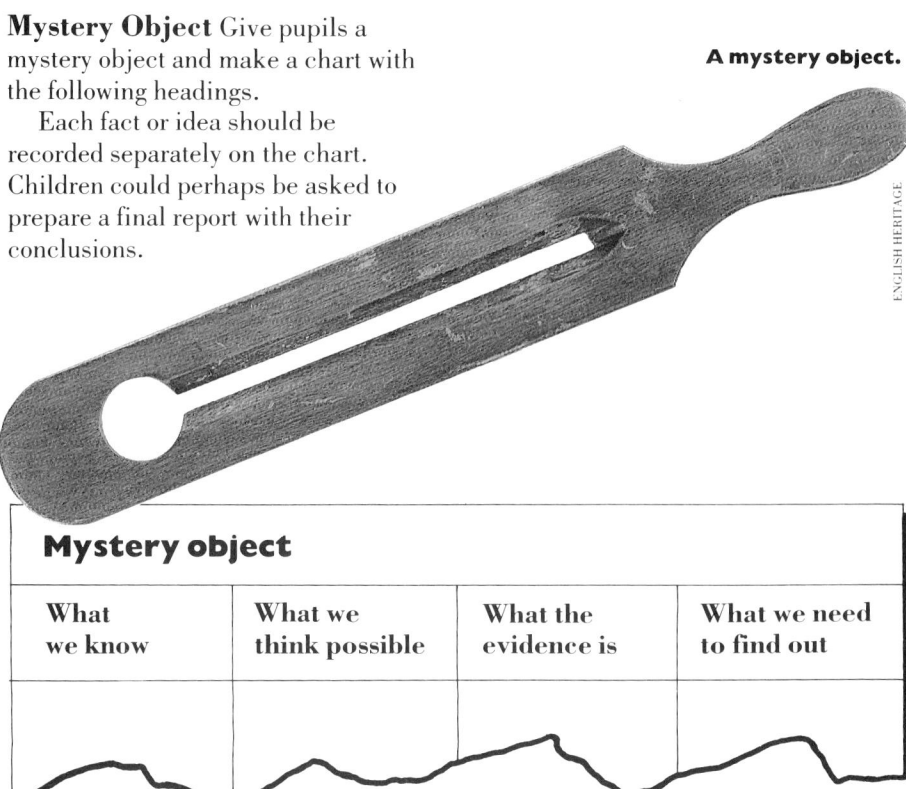

A mystery object.

Mystery object

What we know	What we think possible	What the evidence is	What we need to find out

The Left Luggage Mystery Fill a suitcase with a variety of objects. Pretend that it has been abandoned at a left luggage office. The task of the pupils is to reconstruct the life of the person who left it there. What can they be certain about and what may be true? Discuss how this reflects the problems of dealing with historical evidence.

LEARNING TO USE FRAGMENTS

The archaeologist works from fragments. Broken pottery, pieces of bone, bits of building materials are all used as evidence to reconstruct life in the past. The evidence is fragmentary in other senses too. It is partial because materials have rotted and also because associated traditions and customs may have been largely transmitted by word-of-mouth. Children working in museums or at sites will often be dealing with fragmentary material. They can usefully learn that fragments can yield more information than might at first be expected.

The Broken Plate Prepare three boxes. One should contain a whole china plate with a design on it, the next should contain half an identical broken plate and the third a small rim fragment of the same plate. Give each group one of the boxes. They should not reveal its contents to the other groups. Each group should then examine their pottery and record everything they can discover from it. Discuss with the class what each group has found out. This activity should show that a fragment will often reveal almost as much information as a complete item and it will sometimes provide more; for instance, the nature of the clay can only be seen clearly in the broken pieces.

The remains of these seventeenth-century pots from Beeston Castle are fragmentary but it is possible to get a very clear idea of them from these fragments.

DEVELOPING SKILLS

Completing the Picture Make a collection of coloured pictures from magazines. Cut out a hole in the middle of each picture. Glue the pictures to sheets of white paper. The children have to draw in the missing part, reconstructing the picture from what remains. This exercise shows that you do not have to have the whole of something to be able to decide what the rest looked like. You could discuss how your reconstruction will vary in accuracy according to the amount of evidence that survives.

This dustbin can be used to piece together information about the family who generated the rubbish.

Skeleton Game One child volunteers to 'die' and lies down on the floor. He or she may choose to be buried with a favourite possession. The rest of the children have to decide what would remain in 500 years' time.

The activities suggested in this chapter should be fun to do, but pupils must see them as more than games. Discuss where and when the future applications might be. If you can teach your pupils to draw on these skills automatically when need arises, they will be well equipped to deal with visits to sites and museums and to use objects as sources of knowledge and ideas.

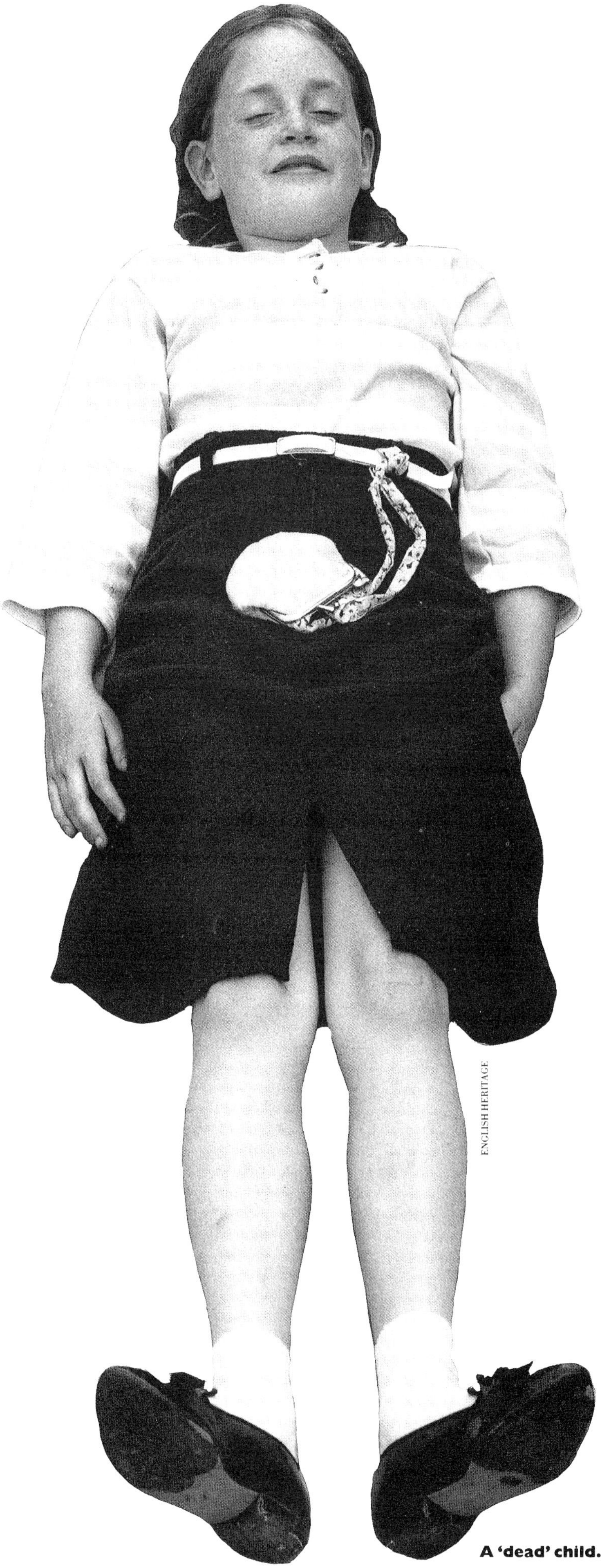

A 'dead' child.

THINKING ABOUT THINGS

This book has emphasised the importance of observation; all analysis and deduction should stem from it and be based upon it. In this chapter we move from the visible to the abstract to deal with the selection of objects and issues relating to their use.

CHOOSING OBJECTS

Select the objects to use according to the points you want to make. Certain categories of object have particular strengths and weaknesses.

■ Uniformly shaped, undecorated or other simple objects, eg. a flat round dish, may look easy to describe initially, but their plainness can make it very hard to hypothesise about function or use owing to the lack of clues.

■ Familiar household items have plenty of potential and need not be discounted. They can be touched, and they demonstrate the excitement of being able to see something ordinary with new eyes, and to see what everyone else will miss.

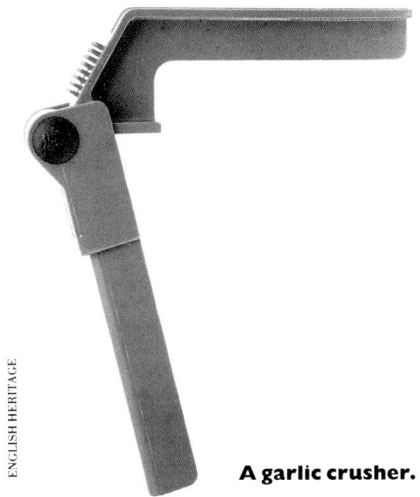

A garlic crusher.

■ Dirty, damaged and worn objects are useful in providing opportunities to talk about concepts of wear and tear, care or neglect, deliberate damage and conservation. Broken objects allow you to look at the inner surface or at their construction, and to practise working out what the whole thing looked like.

This is a Roman mortarium. The fragment on the right could have been used to work out almost as much as the complete dish. The diameter of the bowl could be measured by matching the curve of the rim to pre-drawn circles of known diameter. The grit inside the bowl was clearly placed there deliberately after the pot was shaped since it is not found throughout the clay. The spout suggests pouring or some kind of food preparation and the rough surface inside suggests grinding. The maker's mark is stamped on the rim.

■ Unfamiliar objects immediately evoke in us the desire to know what they are. Unfamiliar objects are of particular use in encouraging people to use their skills of observation and deduction.

■ Some objects have things written on them such as their country of origin, trade marks, details of copyright or registration of design, or even their name. Some things, like pottery, can have a date on them. It may be better to avoid such items initially so that children can develop confidence in their ability to decode an object without falling back on the written word. Later they can start to question the accuracy and importance of the written information. Similarly, some objects come with a known history. A plate may have been grandmother's wedding present or an object may have been found in a particular place. This is all important evidence and its accuracy and significance needs consideration, but again too much emphasis on this type of information at an early stage can undermine the ability to deal with objects without a known history.

USING REPLICAS OR ORIGINALS

The objects you use need not always be originals. Replicas may sometimes be more appropriate, and you need to think about the advantages and disadvantages of each.

Originals may show evidence of wear and tear which provides vital information about the artefact, whereas a replica may not. Originals also help to develop a concept of age, and of chronology. They provide some pupils with a thrill of excitement that no replica can achieve.

Costume is an area where the use of replicas offers great benefits. The fragile and perishable nature of historic costume means it is vulnerable to any sort of handling. This set of costume from the education centre at Osborne House was copied from a photograph of Queen Victoria's children. Only by trying on a well-made replica costume can the detail of the cut be fully understood.

Replicas, on the other hand, can allow pupils to handle and test objects which otherwise could only be looked at. Inaccurate replicas are no less useful than fastidious copies, because they test a pupil's ability to observe and deduce accurately. Signs of wear or dirt in an unlikely place, anomalous or inappropriate materials of construction (eg. a plastic axe or zip in an 'Elizabethan' bodice) should become evident to them. Replicas or fakes can tell you about what someone thought (or thinks) worth replicating, about fashion, about the cost of an object, or about the differences between the unique and the mass-produced.

CONSERVATION

Some classroom discussion of the methods of and reason for conserving objects is a useful preliminary to visiting objects in museums. Museums aim to conserve their collections into infinity whilst at the same time making them available for display and study. All objects are deteriorating; some, like textiles and paper, at a faster rate than others, such as bronze or pottery. Conflicts arise between display and conservation and compromises have to be reached. Objects have to be protected from strong light, the acid on our fingertips, humidity from our breath and the dust that we create, all of which can be very frustrating when we want to get close to something and touch it. Children might consider why we should bother to conserve items, how those objects might be selected, and whether such conservation and preservation should be publicly funded.

VIEWPOINT

Different people 'see' things differently. Your ethnic origins, gender, previous knowledge and experience will all influence the way you perceive things, respond to them, and learn from them.

Ethnic origins The way you perceive certain things is strongly influenced by the customs, traditions, manners and beliefs of the society you have been raised in. Religious artefacts illustrate this point: what is holy to one person may mean nothing to another. A totem pole, which is a sacred object to the people who made it, would represent completely different things to an anthropologist or a carver of wood. Colour is also perceived differently: purple was the imperial colour in ancient Rome but it was the colour of mourning in Victorian England; yellow was the colour of persecution for the Jews in Nazi Germany but saffron is a holy colour to Buddhists.

Customs and traditions can also be used to show how artefacts have different meanings to people of different cultures. Take wedding rituals, for example, and ask the children to name the objects they associate with the word 'wedding', or to bring in photographs which show them. A wine glass forms an essential part of a Jewish wedding ceremony but its symbolism (breaking it represents the end of virginity) would escape someone who had never been to a Jewish wedding; they would view it in a completely different way.

Discussing an object in the classroom.

Gender There are several aspects to this which may prevent pupils from learning from objects. First, it is possible to misinterpret objects from the past by imposing twentieth-century views so that, for example, it is sometimes assumed that prehistoric men used the hand axes and prehistoric women used the bone needles. There is no evidence for this.

The Indian Hindu marriage ceremony of Kalash. The copper pot containing water, representing one of the four elements, is carried by the next female in line to be married on the bride's side. The swastika is a sign of good luck and always used at important ceremonies.

Because objects have been associated with one sex in the recent past we should not assume the same was true in the distant past. In some cases occupations have been the preserve of one sex at one period and then been taken over by the other. Secretarial work was done by men in the sixteenth century although today it is an occupation generally filled by women.

The design of this 1875 typewriter gives very clear messages about who might be expected to use it and in what circumstances. The cover and decoration suggest domestic use and the floral design suggests a female user. Attitudes to typewriting have gone through different phases. In the 1930s it was not unusual for a man to train to be a typist. In the 1950s it was seen as almost exclusively female work, but now the micro-chip has made 'keyboard skills' acceptable to both sexes once more. Boys today might take more interest in this object than they would have done 20 years ago.

Second, if boys think something is sissy, or girls think of something as made for or used by boys, it might actually prevent them from looking at the object or handling it in case it challenges their self-image or the image they wish to present to their peers. Take a flat-iron for instance. If a boy decides that it was something made for and used by women, this not only might prevent him from looking at it properly and discovering that it was a tailor's tool rather than a domestic one, but might also prevent him from assessing its design and function. Pupils need to discuss whether anything can ever be categorised as an implement for a man or a woman and how such categorisation can influence their views of the artefact. Once they have decided that an object was made for a man or a woman they are in danger of bringing all their own ideas about men and women (what they can/can't do, should/shouldn't do, etc.) to bear on the artefact.

Previous knowledge and experience How can your previous knowledge of something affect the way you see it? Many things are so familiar that you simply don't see them any more, and when faced with an ordinary everyday item, you may miss vital clues. Moreover, your previous knowledge of something can stop you thinking freely about it: if you have a jug and recognise it as such, you might assume straight away that it was used as a container for liquids and so miss the vital clues suggesting that it had actually been used for holding flowers or pins or buttons.

On the other hand children, whose previous knowledge and experience is inevitably limited, may not register the significance of an item that conjures up a host of images in the mind of an older person. An older child or an adult can make comparisons and judgements which a younger child cannot. They have a wider context into which to slot an object and a greater familiarity with such things as the materials it is made from or the kind of society which produced it. A child with experience of using craft tools or particular domestic objects may be able to offer important insights into similar objects and their design.

WORTH/VALUE

Another thing which can dramatically affect the way children see something and learn from it is their perception of its value and worth. At a very simple level it affects the way they handle and care for an object but it can also affect the way they look at it. 'Valuable' things, or the things children perceive as 'valuable', seem to merit more attention than those they perceive as 'worthless'.

Children are fascinated by how much things cost; it is a question that they always ask. The topic can raise all sorts of issues. Why do people look after things that they don't actually like, if they happen to be worth a lot of money? Would you buy something you didn't like if you were told it would be a good investment? Have you ever not bought something as a present because you thought it was too cheap? Do you ever buy the more expensive brand of a product because you think it will be better?

If children are going to discuss the monetary value of an object encourage them to do so in context. Give a figure meaning by relating it to a year's earnings or the price of a loaf of bread.

BIAS

What do we mean by 'bias'? It is often taken to imply active prejudice in the thoughts of a person, or a deliberate intention to mislead such as in propaganda. There is, however, another kind of bias, not linked to the deliberate intention to mislead. In this second sense bias means the way each individual or society is different from all others. Upbringing, health, education, relationships, social forces and knowledge give people their different viewpoint or bias.

Old museum display at Lindisfarne Priory.

This Utility radio issued during the Second World War will have strong associations for anyone who lived through the period that may elude a younger person.

New museum display at Lindisfarne Priory. What messages do the different methods of display put across to the viewer?

The creation of a fake, designed to delude people about its real monetary worth, would be an example of the first type of bias. But objects themselves cannot deliberately mislead about their true nature, origins and significance. They are not capable of conscious thought themselves, so they themselves cannot introduce this form of bias.

Artefacts *can* be biased in the second meaning of the word, because any single artefact will be different from all others of its kind. The culture which produces it creates its own bias in the object by affecting the choice of material, the design and whether it is made or not. If you only have one artefact, and no others of its kind to compare it with, you have to be aware of the potentially biased information you are receiving.

For example, if you are studying a single knife, you can make certain deductions about its design, function, manufacture, condition, and so on. However, because you have only one, you must not be tempted to assert certain other things, which the nature of this single object — its bias — might lead you into. Because you only have one, you cannot say how typical this object is of its time, or of its type. You cannot tell whether its state of preservation is normal for a thing of that age, or worse or better; or whether the decoration is particularly sparse or elaborate in this instance; or whether there were other accompanying parts now missing. You can make hypotheses, and then you must either stop until further evidence is available, or do comparisons with other known examples.

In this connection, it will be important to discuss with pupils the circumstances that might determine whether some objects are likely to survive through time more than others. For example, artefacts conceived to be valuable in monetary terms are often preserved long after their utilitarian or original decorative value has gone, and may then be found in an antique collection. Artefacts from upper-class levels of society may be more durable and more carefully preserved than from poorer ones. Some materials survive better than others. Organic materials in particular will often have gone. Thus from prehistoric society we have bones and stones but little idea of make-up and cooking methods, and only a limited knowledge of jewellery, fabrics and dwellings. Archaeological remains frequently consist of the more durable compounds, whilst the more fragile ones can decompose without trace.

CHRONOLOGY

Teachers may want to use objects to develop a sense of chronology. Objects can be sorted into the order in which they were made and possibly also the order in which they were used or acquired, which could be different. Children can look for signs of age, decay, wear, damage, use. They will also have to draw on their personal knowledge and experience. John West's work (see Bibliography) has shown that even infants can learn to do this and collaboratively arrive at proposed sequences supported by reasonable evidence.

Dating objects is a different activity altogether. It often requires very specialised knowledge and considerable experience in handling items, and may rely on information about context which is not available in the classroom. You may find it easier to avoid the question 'How old is it?' in favour of 'Is it older or more recent than x?', which will encourage children to look critically in order to support their ideas.

CONTINUITY, CHANGE AND PROGRESS

Objects provide graphic illustration of continuity and change. The classic typological displays of flint tools, policemen's helmets or embroidered samplers are based on demonstrating the changes and similarities to be found over the course of time. You can also use objects in a more challenging way. Ask why changes have occurred and why objects have become obsolete. Why do miners no longer use Davy lamps? Why did the penny farthing go out of production? Why do we no longer use feather mattresses? How much time passed between changes? Why? Changes are never isolated. Children can look for the causes and the consequences. Why were gas cookers introduced? What effect did this have on home life, women, the design of houses, cookery and cooking equipment?

Objects show that progress does not necessarily mean benefit. Lead pipes brought people water supplies but also poisoned them. Double-glazed windows cut out draught but create new problems of condensation. A change on one front may cause several fresh problems which have then to be solved.

A collection of domestic items recovered from the Mary Rose, a Tudor ship sunk off Southampton. Objects can be dated more easily when found in context and a collection of objects found together is especially valuable as evidence but still needs to be treated with caution. The candlestick was found at the site of the Mary Rose but is of a later date.

RESOURCES AND BIBLIOGRAPHY

OBJECTS TO USE

There should be no difficulty in finding objects to use with your pupils. Sources of objects might be:

The school, your home and garden, the junk shop or the community Local elderly people and collectors may be willing to bring less familiar objects into school and talk about them to pupils.

Museum loan service You may be fortunate in having a museum loan service in your area. You can sometimes borrow a box of items on a specific theme or you may be able to select from a range of individual objects. Contact your local museum to enquire. The service might be run by them or by your LEA. Find out whether they have a catalogue and what the booking and delivery systems are. You may have to collect loans for yourself or they may be delivered. The loan period may be anything from a week to half a term.

Museums and sites Your local museum may be able to offer a variety of activities such as handling sessions, drama activities, GCSE and Standard Grade sessions, slide lectures, drawing and problem-solving activities. Speak to the staff concerned and make a preliminary visit. If a member of the museum staff will be teaching the lesson, discuss the preparatory work that you have done and explain the aims of your visit.

English Heritage has a number of sites with education rooms that are equipped with period and replica items for children to use. See below for address.

FINDING OUT ABOUT OBJECTS

Courses Your local museum's education service may run courses on objects. Phone and ask; suggest one if nothing is on offer or organise one through your Local Education Authority adviser. It may be possible to run something in co-operation with the local teachers' centre. National and provincial museums often have free mailing lists for events and education services.

Identification service Your local museum will run an identification service. Make contact to discover the system they operate. Try to find a member of staff who will deal sympathetically with young people, who can then be encouraged to make use of the service for themselves.

Museum information service Your local museum may have a photograph collection and possibly its own archives. Some museums have published catalogues of part of their collections; others will have unpublished indexes. Always make an appointment.

Museum shop Look carefully at the stock of your local museum shop for books to help you identify objects

Children trained to analyse objects in the classroom find their skills can be transferred to glass-case museums where they cannot handle the objects.

RESOURCES AND BIBLIOGRAPHY

and find out more about them. **Shire Publications** produce an inexpensive series called **Shire Albums** on topics such as kitchen equipment, tools, bottles; their archaeological series provides useful introductions.

Contact:
Shire Publications
Cromwell House
Church Street
Princes Risborough
Aylesbury
Buckinghamshire HP17 9AJ
Tel: 084 444301

Local library The collecting section in your local library will be a helpful source of information and the reference library will probably have a list of societies to help you make contact with local collectors and specialised clubs.

Clubs There may be clubs run by your museum, the Young Archaeologists Club or Young NADFAS (National Association of Decorative and Fine Art Societies) that your pupils could join.

Contact:
Young Archaeologists Club
4 Clifford Street
York YO1 1RD
Tel: 0904 611944

Young NADFAS
8A Lower Grosvenor Place
London SW1W 0EN
Tel: 071-730 3041

The **Group for Education in Museums** is the organisation for all concerned with the educational use of museums, galleries and sites. There is a quarterly newsletter, an annual journal (**Journal of Education in Museums**) and a bibliography. A residential course is held annually and there are regional meetings throughout the year.

Contact:
Susan Morris
Secretary, GEM
63 Navarino Road
London E8 1AG
Tel: 071-249 4296

The **Museums Association** aims to promote and develop museums and art galleries. It publishes the **Museums Yearbook** which lists all museums and galleries and is a useful source of contact names and addresses. You should find a copy in your local library. Within museums there are a number of specialist groups (eg. Social History Curators Group; Women, Heritage and Museums; Science and Technology Curators Group) each of which has its own publications and runs courses. Details of meetings are published in the Museums Association's **Museum Journal** published monthly.

Contact:
The Museums Association
34 Bloomsbury Way
London WC1A 2SF
Tel: 071-404 4767

English Heritage opens over 350 sites to the public, protects historic buildings and ancient monuments, and funds building conservation and rescue archaeology. It has an Education Service that publishes material for teachers, runs courses, establishes education rooms at sites and organises events. **Remnants,** published termly by the Education Service and distributed to all schools in England via the LEAs, contains practical examples of the use of sites.

Contact:
English Heritage Education Service
Keysign House
429 Oxford Street
London W1R 2HD
Tel: 071-973 3442/3

There are separate organisations responsible for historic buildings and monuments in Wales, Scotland and Ireland.

Contact:
Education Manager
CADW
Brunel House
2 Fitzalan Road
Cardiff CF2 1UY
Tel: 0222 465511

Education Officer
Historic Scotland
20 Brandon Street
Edinburgh EH3 5RA
Tel: 031-244 3096

Department of the Environment
(Northern Ireland)
Historic Monuments and
Buildings Branch
Archaeological Survey
66 Balmoral Avenue
Belfast BT9 6NY
Tel: 0232 661621

The Historic Royal Palaces

Contact:
Education Officer
Hampton Court Palace
East Molesey
Surrey KT8 9AU
Tel: 081-977 7222

The National Trust

Contact:
Education Manager
The National Trust
36 Queen Anne's Gate
London SW1H 9AS
Tel: 071-222 9251

Education Adviser
The National Trust for Scotland
5 Charlotte Square
Edinburgh EH2 4DU
Tel: 031-226 5922

The Council for British Archaeology

Contact:
Education Officer
Council for British Archaeology
The King's Manor
York YO1 2EP
Tel: 0904 433925

Tile from Byland Abbey

33

BIBLIOGRAPHY

Since rather more has been written in North America on the use of artefacts than in Britain, a number of the references here are to American and Canadian publications. The British Library has a service for obtaining copies of articles from journals and you should approach your local or college library to gain access to this service.

Getting going

Adams, C and Millar, S, 'Museums and the use of evidence in history teaching', **Teaching History** 34, pp 3-6, 1982. Covers the value of museum visits and the nature of artefacts as historical evidence.

Clarke, P, 'What does archaeology have to offer?', pp 9-12 in Cracknell, S and Corbishley, M (eds), **Presenting archaeology to young people,** Council for British Archaeology Research Report No 64, 1986, ISBN 0-906780-61-6. Suggests ways of dealing with fragmentary archaeological material.

Corbishley, M, 'Not much to look at', **Remnants** 1, pp 1-2, 1986. How to start the hunt for clues.

Corbishley, M, 'The case of the blocked window', **Remnants** 2, pp 1-4, 1986. How to work out the order in which parts of a building or feature were made, introducing the concept of stratigraphy.

Corbishley, M, 'Miss... please miss, why did people live underground?', **Remnants** 3, pp 1-3, 1987. Drawing conclusions from the remains of buildings such as wall footings.

Corbishley, M, 'Coping with the bird's eye view', **Remnants** 4, pp 5-7, 1987. How to bring plans of sites and buildings to life for children.

Corbishley, M, 'Play the skeleton game', **Remnants** 8, pp 8-9, 1989. The source of our Skeleton Game.

Corbishley, M, 'Play the dustbin game', **Remnants** 9, pp 12-13, 1989. Develops ideas for using modern rubbish to help children understand archaeological principles.

Department of Education and Science, **A survey of the use some schools in six Local Education Authorities make of a museum service,** HMI Report, DES 53/87.

Derbyshire County Council, **The blue box: an experiment in time,** Derbyshire County Council, 1987.

Grinder, A L and McCoy, E S, **The good guide: a sourcebook for interpreters, docents and tour guides,** Ironwood Press, Scottsdale, Arizona, 1985, ISBN 0-932541-00-3. Has a helpful section on asking questions.

Jones, M F and Madeley, R A, **Using objects to learn: visual awareness and language development in the classroom,** Royal Ontario Museum, 1983. Has an excellent practical approach and has been drawn on heavily for this book.

Morris, S, **A teacher's guide to using portraits,** English Heritage, 1989, ISBN 1-85074-231-6.

Reeve, J, 'Education in glass case museums', **Journal of Education in Museums** 2, pp 1-6, 1981. Suggests ways of working with displays of material which cannot be handled.

Shuh, J H, 'Teaching yourself to teach with objects', **Journal of Education (Nova Scotia Department of Education)** 7(4), pp 8-15, 1982. The best introduction to teaching with artefacts. We have taken and adapted '50 ways to look at a Big Mac box' from it.

Steane, J, **Archaeology in the countryside,** Council for British Archaeology, Archaeology for Schools series, CBA, 1982, ISSN 0262-897-X.

Thomas, O (ed), **Teaching with overseas artifacts: an interim report from Henley/Boroma Artifacts Group of teachers from schools in the Henley area; on work carried out in class with everyday objects and artifacts from Somalia,** Oxford Development Education Unit, 1983.

Primary case studies

Cross, T and Gosling, N, 'A practical workshop for 7-11 year olds', **Teaching History** 46, pp 28-32, 1986.

Davis, J, 'Artefacts in the primary school', **Teaching History** 45, pp 6-8, 1986.

Dingsdale, A, 'Talking about the past', **Primary Teaching Studies** 2(1), pp 22-36, 1986.

Johnson, T (ed), **In touch with the past: a practical approach to primary history,** Resources for Learning Development Unit, Avon County Council, 1983. Obtainable from Resources for Learning Development Unit, Monks Park Lower School, Sheridan Road, Horfield, Bristol BS7 0XZ.

Wright, D, 'A small local investigation: archaeology and school children', **Teaching History** 39, pp 3-4, 1984. Based on work done as the result of finding broken pottery under the school hedge.

West, J, **History 7-13: guidelines, structures and resources, with 50 classroom**

examples, Dudley Metropolitan Borough, 1981. This major piece of work resulted from four years' research with over 30 Dudley primary schools. Stress is placed on the use of primary sources to develop historical understanding and objects are used extensively to develop a concept of chronology. Many useful strategies are described.

West, J, 'The evidence in hand', **Journal of Education in Museums** 6, pp 41-44, 1985.

Secondary case studies

Davies, J, 'A walk back through time', **History Resource** 2(1), pp 18-19, 1988. Describes an exhibition of objects brought into school by children.

Jeremy, D, 'From a Victorian scrapheap, or an exercise in integrating classroom and museum activity for 14-16 year olds', **Teaching History** 27, pp 10-12, 1980. A proposed scheme of study of nineteenth-century industrialisation closely linking a museum visit with classroom activity and syllabus work.

Reid, A, 'Archaeology in the cause of mixed-ability history', **Teaching History** 32, pp 15-17, 1982.

Loan services

Department of Education and Science, **A survey of how some schools in five Local Education Authorities made use of museum loan services,** HMI Report, DES 290/87.

Sorrell, D, 'Loan services', **Journal of Education in Museums** 1, pp 26-28, 1980.

Examples of studies based on artefacts

Baxter, A, **Discovering nineteenth century fashion,** Hobsons, 1989, ISBN 1-85324-039-7.

Copeland, T, 'The archaeology of education', **Council for British Archaeology Education Bulletin** 4, pp 10-18, 1988.

Girouard, M, **Life in the English country house,** Yale, 1978, ISBN 0-300-02273-5. A very readable exemplar of how the careful study of the design and layout of one kind of building can be made to reveal quantities of information about the society that built it.

Schlereth, T J, **Artifacts and the American past,** American Association for State and Local History, Nashville, USA, 1980, ISBN 0-910050-47-3.

Schlereth, T J (ed), **Material culture studies in America,** American Association for State and Local History, Nashville, USA, 1982, ISBN 0-910050-67-8, which contains Fleming, E M, 'Artifact study: a proposed model' and Gilborn, C, 'Pop pedagogy: looking at the Coke bottle'.

Learning from artefacts

Durbin, G, 'Evaluating learning from historical objects', pp 12-13 in Hooper-Greenhill, E, **Initiatives in Museum Education,** Department of Museum Studies, University of Leicester, 1989, ISBN 0-9515005-0-3.

Fertig, B C, 'Historian/Artifacts/ Learners: the history museum as educator', **Museum News** (USA) 60(6), pp 57-61, 1982. A brief report of a colloquium held in the United States in 1981 where an analysis of the differing roles of artefacts in learning was attempted.

Greenglass, D I, 'Learning from objects in a museum', **Curator** 29(1), pp 53-66, 1986.

Herbert, M, 'Concept-building through objects', **Journal of Education (Nova Scotia Department of Education)** 7(4), 1982.

Hodgkinson, K, 'How artefacts can stimulate historical thinking in young children', **Education 3-13** 14(2), pp 14-17, 1986.

School visits

Pond, M, 'Recreating a trip to York in Victorian times', **Teaching History** 39, pp 12-16, 1984.

Pond, M, 'School history visits and Piagetian theory', **Teaching History** 37, pp 3-6, 1983.

Pond, M, 'The usefulness of school visits: a study' **Journal of Education in Museums,** 6, pp 32-36, 1985.

Richardson, R, 'A new look at the "Educational Visit"', **Education 3-13** 11(2), pp 18-21, 1983.

Slides

The BBC has produced a very useful slide pack to accompany its series **History lost and found.** The twelve slides show objects as diverse as toys and a Kentucky Fried Chicken box and the carefully written notes produced by Sallie Purkis guide the teacher through the kinds of questions to ask to extract ideas and information from the objects. Obtainable from: School Orders, Michael Benn Association, PO Box 234, BBC Schools Publications, Wetherby, West Yorkshire LS23 7EU, tel: 0937 541001.

The English Heritage shop at Stonehenge.

ACKNOWLEDGEMENTS

We are grateful to the following people for help in producing this book: Mary Bryden, Sue Burton and pupils at Ripple Road Junior School, Barking, Patrick Holliman and the pupils of Redlands Primary School, Stepney, Eilean Hooper-Greenhill, Hazel Moffat, Sallie Purkis, Jill Reed, John Reeve, John Hennigar Shuh, Katrina Siliprandi, Anne Teer, Robert Teer, Debra Wilkinson and pupils at Durrington Middle School, and Richard Wood.

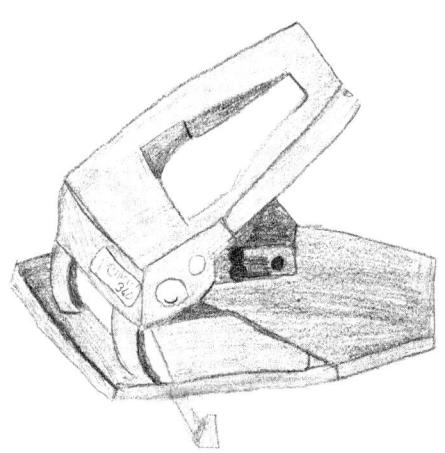

DURRINGTON MIDDLE SCHOOL

A hole-punching machine. Russell Galvin age 9.